ALPHA CROWNES PUBLISHING LTD
Gender Studies

Publisher/Editor
Alpha Crownes Publishing Ltd
107 Windmill Street
Rochester, United Kingdom
in conjunction with
Department of the Performing Arts
University of Ilorin, Nigeria

A catalogue record for this book is available from the British Library.

First published by Alpha Crownes Publishing Gender Studies Series in 2018

Price per copy: £19.99 / N10,000.00 (plus postage)

ISBN 978-0-9935781-4-4

Printed by

Oludolapo Ojediran & Oluwatomi Adeoti (eds.)

CRITICAL PERSPECTIVES ON FEMALE NIGERIAN WRITERS

Alpha Crownes Gender Studies

2

CONTENTS

3

INTRODUCTION

CRITICAL PERSPECTIVES ON NIGERIAN FEMALE WRITERS

Since the 1970s, a significant number of women have engaged themselves with the discussion of female identity, its stability and the meaningful roles of woman within the Nigerian society. Recognised writers like Zulu Sofola, Stella Oyedepo, Zainab Alkali, Mabel Evwierhoma, Irene Salami-Agunloye, Tess-Onwueme, Chima Tracie Utoh-Ezeajugh, Osita Ezenwanebe, Julie Okoh, Onyeka Onyekuba and many others have highlighted female creativity from the feminist angle. As feminism became a fertile ground through which these selected women writers analyse their works, several scholars have researched using different shades of feminism such as black feminism, motherism, STIWANism, femalism, Africana womanism, womanism amongst others. Most female writers agree that sexism and classism are inextricably bound together and cannot be ignored in the exploration of gender discourse. Thus, the feminist theories from different perspectives have helped the black women to feel represented in dominant discourses; to create a self- defined voice for themselves and to discuss their own meaning of womanhood through their own creativities.

Also, the issue of sexualisation and engendering is germane in understanding the socio-cultural importance of the history of gender. This helps to answer the feminist question of how cultural values, linguistic acquisition and patriarchal perspectives interlink with the social forms of gender oppression through the psychological experiences of women. The observations that language is influenced by culture and tradition are important issues that have led to many researches and have been explored by the selected playwrights as this seems to establish the inequalities between the sexes and gives the males greater values than the female ones. This is explained further by Okoh (2003) that as society developed; gender discriminations were institutionalised and reinforced by traditions and religious dogma, until they became part of our cultural heritage. Such gender discrimination lends credence to some values that are coercive, oppressive, enslaving and dehumanising to femalehood, although it claims to command obligations and respect that create a good society at the expense of women. Exclusively, the concern of this book is with the female gender, her language and her identity. Through the understanding of gender, female identity is based on the social subordination and devaluation of the feminine qualities which are often determined by linguistics, environment and pressure towards feminine compliance.

Nevertheless, women narratives come from different perspectives, views, creativities and imaginative domains. Such narratives have been identified to highlight issues of identity construction, engage the society in with setting societal ills and lending their voices as formidable agents in the quest of advancing the society. In this book, female scholars and aspiring scholars examined, interrogated and analysed the works of selected female writers from feminine perspectives. The foci of the writers are on areas that cover different ideologies, narratives, experiences and stories as they seek to nurture, annotate and celebrate female creativity through in-depth language and textual analysis. Issues of culture, religion, aesthetics, gender, sexuality, power, feminism, amongst others, affecting females in the Nigerian system formed the basis of the authors' arguments. The selected plays have been examined as a solution to re-defining femalehood in the patriarchal society by creating females that will act outside the roles to which society has limited them.

In Chapter one, the author discusses language reconstruction and female creativity through which the Nigerian female writer has been able to negotiate the public domain. Chapter twelve analyses two selected works of Tess Onwueme from the socio-political view. Chapters three and four analyze the works of Irene Salami in terms of language, culture and radical conscientisation. Chapter five explores Stella Oyedepo's *Brain Has No Gender*. Chapters six and seven deal with the works of Zulu Sofola who is known as the first published female writer in Nigeria. Chapter eight discusses Julie Okoh's view on femalehood, widowhood and femininity. Chapter nine interrogates gender issues in Tracie Chima Utoh-Ezeajugh's view on patriarchal values while chapter ten views women capacity building towards feminine freedom as a way forward for the female gender. Chapter eleven concentrates on Zainab Alkali's feminist aesthetics in her renowned novel, *The Stillborn*. In Chapter twelve, female subjugation is condemned and feminine energies are explored towards achieving freedom. Finally, chapter thirteen gives an overview of the status and image of the Nigerian women in selected works by different female writers. The intriguing part of this creative venture is that all the chapters are written by females who are writing from the perspective of 'self'. Significantly, the book highlights vital and frequently underrated creative contributions of female writers who have made the Nigerian literary field vibrant and active.

Professor Victoria A. Alabi
Department of English,
University of Ilorin,
Kwara State.

LANGUAGE RECONSTRUCTION AND FEMALE CREATIVITY.

By Oludolapo OJEDIRAN

Introduction

African continent has produced many women writers including Zulu Sofola, Tess Onwueme, Ama Ata Aidoo, Efua T. Sutherland, Ifeoma Okoye, Nadine Gordimer, Stella Oyedepo, Grace Ogot, Bessie Head, Zainab Alkali, Julie Okoh, Sefi Atta and Rose Mbowa who employ their writings to develop ideal opportunities for women to enter the academic and literary world. This creates the means for them to engage in different political, economic, social and cultural discussions that have been male dominated. Most of these women writers use their works at different levels, to explore the politics and dichotomies involved in the female-male relationships at several stages of life. In Nigeria, Salami-Agunloye (2011: 123) observes that, "for many years, Zulu Sofola (1971) was the only female playwright on the Nigerian stage. She was later followed by Tess Onwueme (1983) and Stella Oyedepo, (1982)". These were mainly the female playwrights until other writers such as Catherine Acholonu (1985), Irene Salami-Agunloye (1986) and Julie Okoh (1988) emerged in the late 1980s.

During the 1990s and beyond, other women writers such as Chima Tracie Utoh-Ezeajugh, Osita Ezenwanebe, Onyeka Onyekuba, Bunmi Obasa Julius-Adeoye and Bose Tsevende joined the male dominated domain of creativity. The work of most of these female writers helps to create active reconstruction in the lives of women whereby they can interrogate, navigate and activate their visibility in the public sphere. This collection does not only praise women's essential difference from the patriarchal stereotypes of women, it re-values women's writing and culture which deals with the use of audaciousness as an element in women's language, as portrayed by female writers. The essays in this book explore identity in relation to gender as being culturally constructed rather than being biologically determined which is examined with socially imbibed language. While the essays share the concerns of feminist theory of women's creativity, they also examine the socio-cultural and historic-political functions of women seen through the prism of their language.

Although the theories of gender, language and culture inform a framework of reading works by the female writers, this does not interfere with the interpretations as it goes beyond any of the theories. Accessing the discourse of female writing in the Nigerian society, writers such as Zulu Sofola, Julie Okoh, Stella Oyedepo, Tess Onwueme, Irene Salami-Agunloye, Zainab Alkali, Sefi Atta, Onyeka Onyekuba, Sade Adeniran, Chima Tracie Utoh-Ezeajugh, Osita Ezenwanebe amongst many others question the socio-cultural layout of what it means to be black and female, and what it connotes to be a female writer in a patriarchal society. Through their various themes, these playwrights discover the relationships amongst language, gender and culture. With the creative portrayal of these interlinks amongst the three, the writers recognise that gender as a social construct has incorporated the problem of language, identity and autonomy. The writers' use of language is analysed as an individual's identity beyond the communication of idea. Also, language is presented as the creation of ideas that can also destroy the male gender if not carefully used; and the laid down moral culture that is meant to govern 'self' especially the female gender. Rather than seeing language from stylistic, pragmatics

9

and lexical structure, language in this book is divided into two sub-categories:

i.   Language of power, authority and politics
ii.   Language of ego and sexism

Language Craft in Women's Writings

From the sociolinguistic view, language is governed by social conventions where the social structures account for the meanings of language use which invariably allows women's outward identity to be seen as socially imposed to protect her patriarchal stand. Such patriarchal stand is a gendered attribute which feminist theory hopes to eradicate, to help women perceive themselves as capable human beings rather than accepting themselves as the opposite of men.

This is evidenced by the works of sociolinguists like Robin Lakoff, Dale Spender, Deborah Cameron, Jennifer Coates and Julia Wood who believe that language plays an important role in human communication be it written or oral within the society. As Carby (1987) observes, black women had to confront the dominant domestic ideologies and literary conventions of womanhood that excluded them from the definition of *women* through language to gain public voice as orators or published writers. Although much have been said and written about language, such language tells of the social involvement among human beings within the society and allows them to understand one another.

While Lakoff (1973, 1975) proposes two different styles of language as neutral language and women's language, she also observes that women's language is weak because they use more of question tags, empty adjectives, fillers, qualifiers and other features of women languages. Lakoff (1975: 4-5) identifies the goals in assessing a woman's language as threefold:

> To provide diagnostics evidence from language use on gender inequality; to discuss whether anything can be done on gender inequality from the linguistic end of the problem; and to provide, not the final word on sexism and language, but a goad to further research.

Although Lakoff claims specialised vocabulary, expletives, empty adjectives, tag questions, intonation, super-polite forms, hedges, hypercorrect grammar, joke-telling and humour as introspection and linguistic intuition in women's language, the main criticism of this position is Lakoff's negative evaluation of women's language. She argues that such usage displays elements in their lexical, syntactic and pragmatic use of languages that distinguishes women's speech from that of men's which invariably creates negative effects on women's style of language.

While Lakoff sees language as a sexist medium of representation, her elements of women's language create a sense of exaggerated politeness that make women's language different from men's language. This roughly corresponds to the Danish grammarian, Jespersen's (1922) view that women speak more softly and politely than men, use diminutives, construct their sentences loosely and with hanging phrases and sentences. Jespersen's features of women's speech create the usual stereotype of the female gender which reinforces inequalities and differences in the society as such language make them subordinate to men. Lakoff sees the marginality and powerlessness of women as reflected in the way they use language and societal perception in relation to the female gender. She observes language is a form of prison, specifically a woman's prison to bring out the disadvantaged positions of women from the political and cultural terms. She acknowledges that women are forced to learn a weak, trivial and deferential style of language use as part of socialisation process, therefore making them subordinates.

Lakoff identifies women's language as that form which places women in a subordinate position from early childhood onwards. Although her claim is that women are denied access to powerful style of speech, her work opens further researches to examine whether what she observes is true or otherwise. The search for the differences in women's and men's language use became an emphasis in different research areas as researchers began to respond to the negative historical portrayal of women. This researches challenge some of the sexist tradition that exist between both sexes and their use of language.

During the 1980s, Spender (1980) describes the vast growing body of research on women and language, identifying two specifically different areas. Firstly, she queries differences in language use between men and women based on their sexuality and that if there are, what does that mean to both sexes? Secondly, she observes sexism in language, its effects and the implication on feminist theory. Spender does not limit herself to the celebration of women's writings; she goes further to ask probing questions about the power of language on its users in particular women. She asks if linguistic sexism is the cause and effect of women's oppression and when it appears in language use, if women and men should be speaking different languages or dialects (genderlects), what the boundaries are, and how men control language, if they do? These questions were to challenge feminist criticism to investigate gender differences and to find new relationship amongst gender, language and literature.

In the 1990s, Coates (1998) notes that several studies have dealt with men and women talk in terms of phonological, morphological, syntactic or lexical studies, more works have also been done to show the findings based on conversational analysis. Coates sees language as being deficit, which is the notion of Lakoff's view of women's language as being dichotomous in nature. Secondly, she identifies language as 'dominance' in nature. This sees the extension of deficit approach that gender difference in language reflects power differences in society. Coates also views *difference* as an avenue to gendered speech which shows that men and women belong to different *subcultures*. This is similar to Tannen's (1990) observation about the differences she sees in conversational style between men (report talk) and women (rapport talk).

Tannen reveals the differences in the usage of men and women's language that while men use language as a form of independence, status identification and maintenance in a hierarchical social order, women use language to develop relationships and interactions. Coates' fourth observation sees language from a dynamic or a social constructionist approach. This shows a way of shifting gender or acting gender instead of being gendered. Crawford (1995: 17) affirms that social constructionist approach of language identifies that talk is a power resource brought to bear in influencing other people, enlisting their help, offering companionship, protecting ourselves from their demands, saving face, justifying our behaviours, establishing important relationship and presenting ourselves as having the qualities that they (and we) admire. Putting language and gender in a social constructionist framework often generates lots of questions about gender along with the issue of race, class and age.

Language of power, authority and politics

As an avenue of communication, the feminists see that language interprets the whole of human experience, reducing the indefinitely varied phenomena of the world around people, and the world inside of people. Language has been a powerful metaphor in women's discourse, employed to analyse the ways in which women are denied the rights or given the opportunity to express themselves freely within the patriarchal society. Language as means of communication distinguishes human beings from other living things. The ability to use it with clarity, precision and vividness helps to determine the kind of personality and identifies the social status of the speaker. Language is a major component of any human culture that encodes a culture's preoccupations and its values; it is one of the main means whereby cultures and traditions are transmitted to children and other incomers into the community.

Language and culture are interwoven in creativity; therefore, language becomes an influential force in the shaping of writers' works. It is important for them to use this communication power to their privilege and advantage as its helps to communicate effectively. Spender (1980: 97 points out that:

> people who have the power to use language advantageously have the potential to order the world to suit their own ends, the potential to construct a language, a reality, a body of knowledge in which they are central figures, the potential to legitimate their own primacy, and to create a system of beliefs which is beyond challenge.

This is applicable to female writers who can redress their situation through the use of language in their creation of female characters. For example, in Zulu Sofola's *King Emene,* Obiageli voices out her view that:

> **Obiageli**: What does it matter what my present station in life is? Whether I live or die makes no difference. Suffering is second nature to me and no one knows it better than you. My flesh has become hardened. Your hands have taught me the value of silent suffering intermingled with patience and hope for peace and justice. I believe that one day the truth about the death of my son will be revealed. That day will surely come and these breasts that nursed my son in vain will flow with the milk of joy. My son will rejoice in his grave for at last the untimely and unjust death will have been avenged (p. 8)

Sofola's dramatic language shows the beauty and catchy exploration of woman's language and how they use it to draw people's attention to themselves. In fact, Showalter (1985: 193) observes that it is not language that silences women in the society, but the restriction placed on women's ability or entitlement to use it:

> The appropriate task for feminist criticism is to concentrate on women's access to language. . . on the ideological and cultural determinants of expression. The problem is not that language is insufficient to express women's consciousness but that women have been denied the full resources of language and have been forced into silence, euphemism and circumlocution.

However, the use of positive, creative language by these writers help women to redefine themselves in the society that has limited their ability in history especially in the public sphere where very little is known about women. Showalter (1985: 47-48) notices that:

> The history of England is the history of male lines, not of the female. Of the fathers we know always some fact, some distinction. They were soldiers or they were sailors; they filled that office or they made that law. But of our mother, our grandmothers, our great-grand mothers, what remains? Nothing but a tradition. One was beautiful; one was red- haired; one was kissed by the Queen. We know nothing of them except their names and the duties of their marriages and the numbers of children they bore.

This is noticeable in the works of the Nigerian female writers who present situations whereby marginalisation and suppression within narratives makes it difficult for the women to have self and national autonomy. This mirrors Spender's (1980) view that men have been privileged to be the shapers of cultural forms which include language as the most symbolical of all that has excluded women in the production of cultural forms.

Showalter's (1985) discussion about female writings is a call to female writers to explore the positive aspect of women's cultural position, women's language, women's body and women's psyche through their language. Invariably, this becomes a means of escape for them rather than dwelling on the hierarchical and stereotyped nature that has been identified with women in the society. In Showalter's words, the women writers have found themselves in a sense, without a history; have been forced to rediscover the past anew, forging constantly and consciously into

16

their sex roles that make them very valuable to female literary history.

Importantly, the female writers through their works create determined female characters with roles and situations to help assert their existence in time and history. Evwierhoma (2003) observes that writing is also an avenue of empowerment for women since it enables the female writer to confront all forces threatening to silence her negatively. For example, many of the Nigerian female writers such as Flora Nwapa, Toyin Adewale, Buchi Emecheta and Mabel Segun have been identified to write on impulse to change the status quo, to interrogate patriarchy, imperialism and Western feminism and hierarchy that involve sexist language. Also, that sexist language should not just be considered from what defines, demean or depreciates women, that make them invisible, passive or silent, sexism in language can redefine women to inspire resistance and activeness in any socio-cultural milieu. This shows in Ogunsiji (2013: 23) that language is creative, it is elastic. That the finite rules of language can be used to generate infinite number of sentences because language is not biologically inherited but is socially acquired. However, language is a complex whole which is not independent of culture.

Such writings are to correct their low self-esteem which developed from discriminations and oppressions creating a negative identity in the society. The study of women concerning their language use has a long history which exposes the idea that women and men are treated differently through their use of language. For example, in most of the identified female writers' works, language is viewed as a tool of privilege that gives the male characters the social recognition and importance in the communication hierarchy. Cameron (1995) notes that the rules

17

about language and standards of 'correct speech' reveal information about patterns of power and privilege in the society. Women writers from different cultural backgrounds have shown their concern about the manners in which women are (re)presented in language. Penelope (1990) for example has documented that the early encounters women had with sexist language from St Hildegarde of Brigen in the eleventh century is an attempt to construct an alternative to non-sexist language.

Rather than creating an alternative view on how women's language is identified and treated in the society, Alice Walker (1983) presents the alternative that sexist language could still be used constructively by women and the society by seeing the capability in the female gender. Although in defining sexist language, Weatherall (2002: 10) sees it as not just the words used to describe women, but also how such words are used and to what ends they are being used:

> Challenging sexism in language and making trouble with words can be an important feminist strategy to engender social change. However, it seems to me that the solutions offered to the problem of sexist language are somehow less important than the issue itself. One reason for this is that there is no simple relationship between linguistic forms and non-sexist language.

Weatherall notes that although words can define, depreciate and demean women but at the same time, may also inspire resistance and rebellion against the negative meaning. Thus, sexist language should not just be thought of as constructing women as invisible or passive and silent. This reveals that silence can be used effectively without having a negative connotation as many writers have portrayed it. In some respect, silence is another form of resistance to a domineering culture where the holders of such culture are always ready to checkmate the female activities. Similar to Weatherall's view, Butler (1997: 2) observes that:

> One is simply fixed by the name that one is called. In being called an injurious name, one is derogated and demeaned. But the name holds out another possibility as well: by being called a name, one is also, paradoxically, given a certain possibility for social existence... thus the injurious address may appear to fix and paralyse the one it hails, but it may also produce an unexpected and enabling response.

Butler's observation elaborates the view of some female writers whose works recreate women culturally, mythically, socially, economically, financially and politically within the society that has limited their contributions. They recreate their self to feel great, powerful and highly valued individuals as a means of showing the female worth.

Also, Black and Coward (1998) explain that language participates in the social and has an active role in the construction of its subjects' social statuses. Spender (1980: 52) agrees that language is a weapon that women writers have not been able to use extensively in their fight against sexism. Evwierhoma (2003: 14) confirms that "the woman writer's inability to use language to her own advantage is likely to obtain in a phallocentric society, where female artistry is often socially inhibited. This inhibition could therefore estrange her from the mainstream of writing and limit her contribution". Apart from the corrective measure achieved by female creativity and writings, Driver (1982: 203) expresses her belief that such writings are genuine consciousness created by women to communicate to their audience. Driver thus asserts "literature as means of giving autonomous value to women's experience by helping women perceive the political, economic, and social expression to which women were subjugated as well as attempt to bring about new standards against which women would be measured. Such experiences and perspectives of women mandate their inquiry into historical priority, universality and overriding importance of patriarchy through their different writings.

This expression elaborates Alice Walker's definition of womanism as seeing the capabilities in women. Writing gives women empowerment and freedom to think and feel. Freedom to think and feel are parts of the distinct features of the womanist ideology which allows mental, body and personal autonomy. Through such writings, female identity, female dignity, female protestation and female feminine assertive aesthetics are explored. Eckert & McConnell-Ginet (1998: 485) opine that "women's language has been said to reflect their conservatism, prestige consciousness, upward mobility, insecurity, deference, nurture, emotional, expressivity connectedness, sensitivity to others, solidarity".

Language of ego and sexism

Language, however, could either be an expressive or oppressive tool within the society which could determine the linguistic strength of a gender. McConnell-Ginet (1998: 199) explains that using language is a socially situated action, it is clearly embedded in the same socio-cultural matrix that supports sexual bias in the work we do... the expectations we have of ourselves and others and so on. Therefore, language in the society is introduced as a very powerful and significant indicator of status. While Lakoff (1975: 16) identifies language itself as a tool of oppression because women's speech is often "tentative, powerless and trivial", Spender (1980: 52) observes that historically, women have been excluded from the production of cultural forms, and language is after all, cultural form and a most important one. In awkward terms, this means that language has been made by men, that they have used it for their own purposes. Spender however sees language and gender as being interwoven and interlinked by their correlative development through social and cultural practice.

Although this book considers the assertion, it also explores their opposites to justify womanist view of the 'capability' of females according to Walker (1983). Crawford (1995: 94) identifies this as acting within a social constructionist framework. She agrees that women behave in a certain way not because of their sex, but because they are members of a distinct, culturally salient group who are placed in particular situations and interactions that enable certain behaviours and suppress others. She further asserts that "some girls and boys come to experience intimacy and autonomy differently because the gender system operating at the social, structural and interactional levels recreates the ideology of gender within individuals.

However, language exposes the kind of social being that we are and helps give entry into the patriarchal culture through speech. The problem is that women are marginalised in patriarchal societies, because while men find language as a tool to social entry, women see it as an impossible objective. For most women writers, language is not a tool of recognition of who they are, but a tool of oppression. This reflects Spender's point noted earlier about man-made language and reinforces Deborah Cameron, Jennifer Coates and Deborah Tannen's exploration of written language in particular as an alien concept for women.

Language, like gender, cannot be easily looked upon without reference to socio-cultural factors that determine the perceptions of identity whether personal or national. In line with language creating identity, these women writers do not clamour for a total dissociation from these pasts, but it should be identified as a form of reconstructive continuity that will shape the present. Hence these various factors must be taken into consideration and investigated to some extent in any gender focused discourse analysis. The socio-cultural factors are noticeable in many of their works like Zulu Sofola's *Wedlock of the Gods*, Flora Nwapa's *Efuru*, Mabel Segun's *Under the Mango Tree*, Julie Okoh's *Mannequins*, Buchi Emecheta's *The Joys of Motherhood* and so on. Many of the works produced by these women writers are their personal and social identity; and reflections as writers, as women and as characters in the larger societies. The female characters in their works are portrayed as multi-dimensional agents who no longer remain marginalised and voiceless. For example, in Julie Okoh's *Mannequins*, Mrs. Adudu refuses to be subjugated by the cultural expectation which celebrates a man's infidelity within the African patriarchal society. At the end of the play she realises she has a brighter and better future without a man while she leaves the house to start a new life. This is also visible in Sofola's *Wedlock of the Gods*, when Ogwoma decides to be emancipated after the death of a husband she is forced to marry. She sees it as being limited and voiceless within this culture; she wants her freedom rather than being an unhappy individual throughout her life because of cultural obligation. Ojediran (2013: 58) sees that Sofola creates characters and storyline that are representational; appealing to readers' physicality and emotions.

In line with Okoh and Sofola's view of the female ill treatment in the society, Emecheta (1990: 27) observes the false female characterisation in Chinua Achebe's work which explores the socio-cultural treatment of women in the Igbo community of

Nigeria. Emecheta criticises that "The good woman" in Achebe's portrayal is the one who kneels and drinks the dreg after the husband. In Achebe (1964: 42), when the husband is beating his wife, other women stand around saying "it's enough, it's enough". In his view, according to Emecheta, that kind of a subordinate woman is the good woman. Until recently, culturally for example in some of the Nigerian societies for long time, female children were mainly appreciated because of their monetary value in terms of the price they attract when they get married.

Reading through the works of these Nigerian women writers' such as Ifeoma Okoye, Zaynab Alkali, Teressa Meniru, Lara Daniels, Folake Taylor and Catherine Acholonu, readers see the observations and recommendations of these writers that one of the ways of correcting the faulty image of the Nigerian women is to see from the 'inside', in other words, rendered by women. Although, male writers, including John Pepper Clark-Bekederemo, Femi Osofisan, Bayo Afolabi and Ahmed Yerima, are writing in support of women emancipation, freedom, autonomy, the fact remains that these male writers are writing outside the female body and cannot tell the feminine tales from the feminine view/experience. For example, Ademeso (2009: 29) observes that:

> In Africa today, a discourse on feminism as a literary theory cannot be fully held without giving more attention to the position of Osofisan and his treatment of female characters in his plays. He sees women as opposite of men, not in terms of sex or physical outlook alone; he sees them as partners in progress, who could achieve a lot without being wasteful or corrupt. He sees them as having more

wisdom than men who use aggression or war in conflict resolution…

Osofisan sees women as people in search of knowledge, liberation and self-fulfilment both in history and contemporary times. However, the works from Nigerian women writers highlight the exclusion of women from the public spheres, elaborates domesticity and publicise patriarchy. These three avenues, personal expressiveness, emotion and empathy are means through which Walker's view of womanism allows these women writers to use their writings as an avenue to communicate with other women in the society since writing make up the collation of history. Through language use, Nigerian women writers have tried to redeem women's lost history in the literary world and to attain self-actualisation in their various societies. To a large extent, these writers have been able to correct the bias undertone in the cultural description of women that reinforces them as decorative objects whose identity hinges on physical appeal and not what they contribute to the society positively.

Considering this from their works, female writers' language is a means through which female dignity, femininity, protestation and feminine aesthetics are explored while the constraints affecting female creative impulse is discarded. Cameron (1998: 50) observes that:

> The great change that has crept into women's writing is, it would seem a change of attitude. The woman writer is no longer bitter. She is no longer angry. She is no longer pleading and protesting as she writes. We are approaching, if we have not yet reached, the time when her writing will have no little or foreign influence to disturb it. She will be able to concentrate upon her vision without distraction from outside. The

aloofness that was once within the reach of genius and originality is only now coming within the reach of ordinary women.

Cameron's assertion made twenty years ago, has been an influence in the works of female writers. The use of language both in oral or folktale and written form in these works have created assertive, determined and actualised female roles. For women writers to have been able to use these two forms constructively and effectively show their dynamicity, flexibility, capability and adjustability to the 'male sphere'. Such use of poetic lines and oral forms embrace satirical, overt political and cultural activism that depicts women's plights and collective ethos as well as tools for castigating built in social structures which Kolawole (1997) views as the need of feminine gender by the female poets and dramatists. Apart from writing in different Nigerian languages – Igbo, Yoruba, Efik, Pidgin, or Hausa, for example – the oral narratives and the folklores in these female writings depict their connections with their respective cultures which elaborate their richness of imagination. Showalter (1977) sees that women are been regarded generally as 'sociological chameleons' who take on the class, lifestyle and culture of male counterparts. She argues further about women constituting themselves as a subculture within the framework of a larger society and unifying themselves by values, conventions, experiences and behaviours infringing on everyone. This reveals that there is a gendered use of voice, vocabulary, language, view and knowledge which the female gender adapts to be reckoned with in the society. To this end, this authenticates Simone de Beauvoir (1974: 20) as quoted by Akoh (2015: 159) that "one is not born, but rather becomes, a woman".

Conclusion

Enejere (1991: 49) observes that in Nigeria, "the problem of women looms large. Economic backwardness, ignorance, religious prejudice and obsolete ideas about women's place at home and in society still tell on their position". While Enejere's view is a major concern in the Nigerian society, female writers have tried as much as they can to see that such situations are identified, presented and corrected through their suggested solutions. Such writings surreptitiously influence the society views that these female biological roles are to be used positively and not as limiting key into the social sphere. As these women writers engage in different forms of social mobility, they deal with linguistic aesthetics that revalue their deviated socio-cultural positions. However, this helps them to deviate from the media and masculine representation which has limited them and to create a female gender who is not totally dependent or subservient. It is obvious that more women's works need to be written, showcased, analysed and criticised in the public to promote their involvement in the academic, political, economic, and socio-cultural sphere. This will also help to bring more women's work to the fore front in the literary world.

REFERENCES

Achebe, C. (1989). *Arrow of God.* Herts: Anchor Press.

Ademeso, A. (2009), "The drama and theatre of Femi Osofisan: A critical appraisal". In Emasealu, E. (Ed.), *The CRAB: Journal of Theatre & Media Arts.* Vol. 5, pp. 1-35.

Akoh, D. (2015). "Gender, sexuality and power in select Nigerian drama". In Utoh-Ezeajugh, T.C. & Ayakoroma, B. F. (Eds.), *Gender discourse in African theatre, literature and visual arts. A festschrift in honour of Professor Mabel Evwierhoma.* Ibadan: Kraft Books.

Beauvoir, S. D. (1974). *The second sex*. Hardmondsworth: Penguin.

Black, M & Coward, R., (1998). "Linguistic, social and sexual relations: A review of Dale Spender's man-made language". In Cameron, D. (Ed.) *The feminist critique of language*. London: Routledge.

Butler, J. (1997). *Excitable speech: A politics of the performative*. London: Routledge.

Cameron, D., (1995). *Verbal hygiene: The politics of language*. London: Routledge.

Carby, H. V. (1987). *Reconstructing womanhood: The emergence of the Afro- American women novelist* (6th ed.). New York: Oxford University Press Inc.

Coates, J. (Ed.). (1998). *Language and gender: A reader*. New Jersey: Wiley Blackwell.

Crawford, M. (1995). *Talking difference: on gender and language*. London: Sage Publishers.

Driver, D. (1982). *Feminist Literary Criticism*. New York: Rodopi Publishers.

Eckert, P and McConnell-Ginet, S. (1998). *Language and gender: A reader*. New Jersey: Wiley Blackwell.

Emecheta, B. (1990). *New York Times Book Review*. New York: New York Times Press.

Enejere, E. (1991). "Women and political education". In Chizea, D.O. & Njoku, J. (Eds.), *Nigerian women and the challenges of our time*. Lagos: National Council of Women Society.

27

Evwierhoma, M. (2003). *Female empowerment and dramatic creativity in Nigeria*. Ibadan: Caltop Publications (Nigeria) Limited.

Kolawole, M. (1997) *Womanism and African Consciousness*. Eritrea: African World Press.

Jespersen, O. (1921). *Language: Its nature, development and origin*. Michigan: University of Michigan Library.

Lakoff, R. (1975). *Language and women's place*. Oxford: Oxford University Press.

Ogunsiji, A. (2013). "The power of language", in Ogunsiji, A., Kehinde, A., and Odebunmi, A., (eds.), *Language, literature and discourse*. Ibadan: Sterling-Horden Publishers. pp. 23-36.

Ojediran, O. (2013). "Womanist aesthetics of assertiveness on Zulu Sofola's *Wedlock of the Gods*". *The Performer: Ilorin Journal of the Performing Arts*. Vol. 15; pp. 56-67.

Penelope, J. (1990). *Speaking freely: Unlearning the lies of the fathers' tongue*. Oxford: Pergamon Press.

Salami-Agunloye, I. I. (2011). *Challenging the master's craft: Women playwright in the theatre of men*. Boston: Evergreen Books.

Showalter, E. (1977). *A Literature of their own: British women novelists from Bronte to Lessing*. New Jersey: Princeton University Press.

Sofola, Z. (1974). *King Emene*. Ibadan: Heinemann Educational Books.

Spender, D. (1980). *Man-made language*. London: Routledge and Kegan Paul.

Walker, A. (1984). *In Search of our mothers' gardens: Womanist Prose*. Berkshire: Cox & Wyman Publishers.

Weatherall, A. (2002). *Gender, language and discourse (Women and Psychology)*. London: Routledge.

WOMEN, SOCIO-POLITICAL ISSUES AND THE NIGERIAN EXPERIENCE IN TESS ONWUEME'S *REIGN OF WAZOBIA* AND *TELL IT TO WOMEN*

By Oluwakemi Mercy EMMANUEL-OLOWONUBI

Introduction

Since independence, what we refer to as modern Nigeria has tactically failed to measure up to the idea of an ideal modern state. Nigerians are confronted with several socio-political issues emanating from the spiral of cultural and religious roots, causing diverse crises. These range from leadership management, resource control, inadequate and justifiable representation, non-equitable distributions of amenities, maltreatment and inhuman behaviour by dominant groups against the minority groups, both politically and socially, which also involve gender disparity between men and women in Nigeria.

Despite the ongoing efforts by women and concerned individuals to salvage womanhood from the stigma of inferiority, little progress has been made to restore the dignity accorded women in pre-colonial Nigeria, before the period of British colonialism and Western imperative. At the time, there were numbers of women of virtues whose leadership acumen and charismatic personality were remarkable. Queen Amina of Zazzau, Madam Tinubu of Lagos, Efunsetan Aniwura of Ibadan, Inikpi of Igala Land and Emotan of Benin wielded political, economic and cultural power. These women did not allow their femininity to affect their determination to command kingdoms and influence developmental and diplomatic changes and growth in their immediate and neighbouring communities. In the periods succeeding the era when these women lived, and during the colonial period, women lost their controlling grip in the socio-political facet of life. Subsequently, in recent times, as Akinwale (2011: 291) avers,

> Women in Nigeria are beginning to step out of their cultural shells to excel in their chosen professions. Today, some are managers of big companies and banks, owners and medical doctors of several health clinics, professors in the academia and even presidential candidates of some political parties in the country....

Despite this level of achievement, many still agitate for more inclusion of women in the transformational process of the society especially in the political arena. Imperative to this study is a reading of socio-political implications of feminine projection in the selected plays of Tess Onwueme. These plays explore the issues of women's agitation and at the same time, negotiate socio-political empowerment for women in the male dominated society. The pros and cons of this struggle and its reflections in the society are examined in this chapter.

A Review of Literature

The promotion of gender discourse in the Nigerian society has continued to attract growing attention from both women and men and this is yielding positive results. The movement in all its nomenclatures aims at deconstruction and reconstruction of some perceived injustices necessitated by culture, religion and other social factors. From literary angle, Sotunsa (2008: 8) asserts that:

> Feminist literary criticism confronts patriarchal values. It attempts to unveil the prejudices embedded in the appreciation of arts and cultural artifacts. It also exposes how the linguistic medium promotes

and transmits the values of male domination. Feminism's major aim is to combat female oppression and repression in all forms.

Despite the linguistic reflections of male domineering of the womenfolk above, the manifestation of subjugations and the reactionary trends to right the wrong is everywhere. Therefore, Ezeigbo in *Gender issues in Nigeria: A feminist perspective* (1996: 38) posits that feminism "emerged as a response to oppressive and unjust laws and attitudes arrayed against women. These laws ensured that women remained in subservient, dependent and marginalized positions, permanent relegating them to the background".

This ideology can be viewed as one that arises out of the need for women to liberate and empower themselves from shackles of male domination and oppression. Because of the misconception that men are superior to women, this yardstick has been used to justify and maintain economic, political and social authority by the male. However, Ojediran (2012: p.17) states that, in advancing the identity of womanhood in the society:

> Women need to appreciate their positions not in a passive way, but as a way of creating a variety of recognizable identities for themselves. However, when women express themselves through such an avenue, it depicts their self-articulation and self-determination through aesthetics of assertiveness.

The sense of assertiveness has brought about the fight for self-determination of proper and rightful socio-political, economic and religious place and maintains certain control (rights) over their body in the society. This is supported by Idegu (2009: 77) that women quest for:

Individual autonomy, rights, freedom, independence, tolerance, cooperation, nonviolence and diversity, domestic violence, gender, sexuality, discrimination, sexism, non-objectification, freedom from patriarchy, right to an abortion, reproductive rights, control of the female body… prostitution and education.

Importantly, women within their cultural localities, strive to challenge all factors that limit their urge for political, cultural and social recognition even when such is limited. Hence, their negotiation is not to seek for equality but rather to seek for the overhauling of the social system to honour women emancipation and political integration in African setting. At different times and approaches, these platforms have allowed women to record success in many areas. For instance, especially in Nigeria, these have given some women the chance of holding public offices. Unfortunately, some observable problems have stopped political elevation of women especially in governance; and are attributed to lack of proper sensitisation from the elites to the rural women. This suggests that an education of the disadvantaged rural women can sensitise and awaken the latent consciousness of women to identify and resist injustice against self and others especially as the ability to resist injustice is inherent in our collective psyche. This has earlier been confirmed that "the consciousness to identify injustice against humankind, and particularly women, can be strongly argued to be inborn [...] awaiting some re-awakening and re-focusing to give it broader and deeper followership" (Idegu, 2009: 81). This refutes the misunderstanding that feminism is a borrowed concept from the Western World.

In fact, the naturalness of gender agitation in the time past, especially in Africa is traceable to remarkable strides of women in the society. For instance, it has been observed that:

> Some societies in Africa have had women who ruled kingdoms and led conquest wars (sic). Examples of such recognized cum documented women are Berber queen known as the Kahina of the Maghreb (17th century), Magajiyas of Daura (9th century), Queen Amina of Zazzau (16th century), Nzinga of Angola (19th century), and Nehanda of Zimbabwe (19th century) (Azunwo and Omovwiomo, 2015: 1).

Also, many women such as Madam Tinubu of Lagos and Moremi of Ile-Ile have occupied political positions and ruled large kingdoms, wielding economic and political powers. This shows that women and men are potentially enabled to have the same degree of aspirations. To this, Obadiegwu (2009: 104) notes that:

> Men and women are complimentary opposites in traditional African society. No gender dominates the totality of the social life of the people in African environment. Men are dominant in socio-political spheres of life, while women have the upper hand in the spiritual and metaphysical segments.

Politically in Yoruba history, there have been instances of women reigning as regents of Oyo Kingdom and Ooni (Chief Priest) of the primordial city of Ile-Ife. After Alaafin Aganju died, leaving no heir to succeed him as king, his pregnant queen, Iyayun, reigned as Regent of Oyo until her son became old enough to be king. She wore the crown and put on the royal robes and other royal insignia and ruled the kingdom[1]. The discontinuity of this legacy can be linked to a possible lack of courage of the women to determinedly assert their rights, or to the overbearing patriarchal system of the feudal Yoruba kingdom. The loss of this political grip on power by women especially in modern time calls for all concerned womanist to rebrand gender campaigns beyond the fecund of equality and representation, and to include self-determination and gender restructuring. The laws that inhibit political freedom of women are made by groups of men which in a way has relegated larger segment of women to the background. Women should be courageous enough to activate and mobilize their number to effect the needed political change with a rather consistent persuasion and not intimidatingly.

Women in power corridor and the Nigerian Experience in Tess Onwueme's *Reign of Wazobia*

Since the inception of the Fourth Republic in Nigeria, the political arrangement allows changes in leadership positions every four years at State and National levels. The executive arm of power can be elected for a second term in office whilst the legislative arm enjoys life time tenureship, if they get support from their constituencies. Any attempt however to thwart or overstay in office beyond the constitutional stipulated time incites responsive protest in the concerned stakeholders. Even when the elected leaders should enjoy the constitutional benefits of term extension, due processes are to be followed in a polling system. This is the expected notion of leadership in the country. However, the situation is different in Wazobia by Tess

---

[1] See Johnson, S. (1921; 1960 rpt.), *The History of the Yorubas from the Earliest Times to the Beginning of the British Protectorate*, Lagos: CMS (Nigeria) Bookshops, pp. 155-156.

Onwueme, where the stubbornness and resistance to change by a regent leads to a different outcome.

In *Reign of Wazobia*, at the expiration of a regime because of the death of Ilaa of Anioma Kingdom, the need to inaugurate an interim ruler becomes pertinent to the survival of the political lives of the people. Tradition demands that there be selected a female regent who will reign for three seasons before the selection and instalment of a new king. Wazobia, an educated female, is the new regent who is required to spend three seasons by tradition. At the end of the third season, Wazobia however refuses to relinquish the throne. This is because Wazobia's gender restructuring agenda has not yielded the expected results as men, in their mentality, still reject the progressive future awaiting the women as conceived by Wazobia.

Apart from the fact that Wazobia's constitutional reign has elapsed, her constructive mindset to change the obnoxious practices against women in Anioma kingdom endears her to the public. With the mace of power, Wazobia asserts higher degree of control over the fluffiness of Chiefs like Iyase, in the development of a better and ideal female friendly society. As agent of change, Wazobia remains undeterred from championing the course of womanhood and refuses to be intimidated by negative propaganda. For Wazobia, the task before the women is important and needs urgent attention which centres on total abrogation of all laws and customs that enslave women. She sets her goals in an address with the women of Ilaa.

> **Wazobia**: Women, that is the task before you. To set the hand of the clock aright. To move time, and not allow time to move you… it's our time to till. It's our time to tend that we may be planted on firm soil… (p. 23).

36

Courage and undaunted spirit to resist the ignominy of gender discriminations and subjugation by men within cultural map-out shows her as an emulative leader for Nigerian Female politicians. The lack of political will and spirit of resistance contributed to the fall of a one-time speaker of the House of Representatives, Hon. Patricia Eteh. Her lack of women centred agendas and political machinations led to her catastrophic political downfall. It is sad that Nigerian women unlike women from a few other countries in Africa lack the needed courage to imprint legacies of social change in active political participation as shown in the characterisation of Wazobia. Her display of intelligence power in the management of the crisis eventually turns out to be her selling points against the machinations of the male chiefs.

Unfortunately, the chiefs motivate the youth to demand the implementation of the constitutional provisions that limit regency to three years. In Nigeria, many politicians at the executive arms are limited to two terms in office. However, there is no such provision for the legislative arm, which potentially provides more opportunity for the completion of an agenda or execution of a policy. Wazobia could at the early stage of her reign initiate plans not just to better women conditions, but to adjudicate the ascension and succession of policies that will ensure the eligibility of women to the throne, through the three-year limitation of her regency prevents the full implementation of these.

The action of Wazobia is a progressive attack against the forces of backwardness and by implication, a call for a reform in the mental and sociological presentation of self-esteem in women to create and forge a new personal and social understanding within a patriarchal society. Unlike women politicians in Nigeria especially members of the Women Leaders in Nigeria, Wazobia

37

involves the generality of women (both old and young, literate and illiterates, skilled and unskilled) in collectively challenging the antagonistic male dominant posture to end her reign and remove her regency This is seen as the play opens. Wazobia is heard mobilizing the women of Ilaa:

> **Wazobia**: Arise women!!!
> They say your feet are feeble, show them those feet carry the burden of the womb.
> They say yours are frail, show them those hands have claws, show them those hands are heavy.
> Wake up, women.
> Arise, women.
> Barricade the entrance to the city, I can hear trumpet sounds voice of men spitting blood to drown us.
> With your claws hook them, but spill no blood for these are sons of our womb (p. 2).

The struggle to awake, sensitize and conscientize the women was not easy for Wazobia, as Omu opposes Wazobia's action. Omu, who is regarded as the "king" of the women of Ilaa, advises Wazobia not to overthrow tradition, that she "will not be party to the death of tradition. The ones who hold the titles of the land must hear how you misrule them" (p. 22).

> **Omu**: It is our tradition that women who survive funeral rituals dance in the market place as final mark of their innocence regarding their husband's death. A woman who dies mourning is unclean and must be left to rot in the evil forest (p. 21).

Unlike how Patricia Eteh of the Nigerian legislature and other women who have in one way or the other contested for a political seat have suffered political injustice, onslaught and intimidations from men in the society, Wazobia remains dominant and refuses to surrender out of fear of failure. She refuses to allow intimidation from the men to cloud her maturity as she keeps on sensitizing Omu about the danger associated with some customs and traditions that do not just undermine the glory of womanhood but rather degrade the values of self-rights in the society. Upon awareness, Omu later joins her fellow women to resist the furtherance of male hegemony in matters of tradition.

Addressing the women of Ilaa later, Omu confesses that "Until our great king [Wazobia] opened my eyes I was not aware what heat women steamed in... Thanks to our great king who pulled the veil from MY and YOUR eyes that we may further the cause of women (Reign ..., p. 48). Omu leads a reactionary protest, with nakedness as weapon, to militate men's insurrection against the throne of Wazobia. The protest is also an indication of the end of obnoxious tradition that keeps women subjugated.

Unfortunately, in Nigeria, fallen women who have occupied political offices failed in the struggle against their male counterparts because of their egoistic-operandi of alienation which distance their co-women and the larger society of women. In March 2017, Senator Ali Ndume from Bornu State was suspended for six months by the Senate committee on ethics and privileges for calling for a probe into allegations involving the Senate President. Ndume's people went to the National Assembly to protest the decision of the Senate. On the contrary, there was no such movement in support of Patricia Eteh when she was removed as the Speaker of the House of Representatives, despite being the first woman to hold that post in the political history of the country. This is perhaps because the victim had excised herself from the 'umbilical cord of womanhood' when elected into the House. Another point in favour of Wazobia is that she, despite her level of education, do not undermine the power of the rural and traditional women in the struggle against the bourgeoisie men in the culture bounded society. Her malleable personality makes her to easily appeal to women:

> **Wazobia**: They want Wazobia ousted, Wazobia too resists and will persist. I Wazobia will show them what the left hand did to the anus. I am the earth itself where will you move it to? I Wazobia have tasted power and WILL NOT GO (p. 6)

Wazobia's refusal to quit the throne exacerbates men's fears and divides the society. One must however understand the agitation of Wazobia and her feminine counterparts as a result of the conduct of the men in the kingdom, and that they have one focus: the betterment of women. For instance, Wazobia believes widows must not be subjected to incessant funeral rites that men under similar situations will not perform.

Socio-cultural Reading of Nigerian Women in Tess Onwueme's *Go tell it to Women*

Go tell it to Women displays loopholes that have been the major impediment to the actualisation of rightful social image for women in the society. It also reveals how the urban literate women especially those with Western cultural expositions, perceive their counterpart at the rural area. The play, according to Mabel Evwierhoma (2013: 173) "is the result of class experimentation… [that] tries to refocus on the feminist ideology and its usefulness within an African community". In this play, women are accused of being their own enemies as portrayed in the character of women like Yemoja, Daisy and Ruth. It is from this ideology that women activate so many programmes to alleviate and elevate the lives of women from poverty and to empower them. However, in contemporary society, women go around in the name of these "Better Life Programmes", creating Non-Governmental Organisations (NGO) to collect funds from different governmental bodies and International NGOs but do not use the funds for the proposed programmes; they fraudulently misappropriate the funds. In other words, this 'urban women' use the 'rural women' as source of attracting funds from world donors by planning and faking the gender problems and poverty to extort this organizations. They usually adopt Top-Bottom approach in relating with the women. For instance, in this play, Daisy and Ruth plan on behalf of rural women without their involvement in the process. They only visit the village to invite them for a Better Life programme to be launched in the city. This unwholesome act can be likened to the serial political failures that easily greet women participation in the Nigerian context. The failure can also be ascribed to disunity among the female movement as character Okei laments this factor among women: "Women! Now you do not fight for equality but for the extermination of every other, including your fellow women!!!" (p. 184).

If politics is a game of numbers, and women constitute almost average of our population, it is noteworthy that women have seldom won absolute majority in the elections. In the last presidential primary elections (2015), one of the leading political parties, the Peoples Democratic Party (PDP), with Sarah Jubril standing against former president Goodluck Jonathan, she only won votes where women were more than half of the delegates. This is because many women politicians adopt Daisy and Ruth's Top-bottom approach instead of Bottom-Top approach. If the delegates have been initiated and enlightened like Wazobia in *Reign...,* they would have been convinced to act otherwise.

This in a way shows intra-gender stratification of women which to an extent demonstrates that women are not just accomplices of gender discrimination but had been the stumbling blocks against the actualisation and stabilisation of gender construct in the society. Also, the display of lack of African integrity in gender relation by Daisy, who is involved in a lesbian relationship with Ruth despite being married to Okei, and the maltreatment of her daughter Bose, is seen not just as abuse of womanhood but degradation of motherism virtues of African feminism.

As a result, the rural women are disappointed with the flagrant, nay, impious display of dishonourable acts of indecency that limits political participation of women in decision making. Therefore, the Better Life programme (as feminism) stands to fail as the rural women, against the urban mentality, realises that they are been treated as fools and subsequently mobilise themselves to demand self-dependency towards empowerment. They thereby insist on being involved in the negotiations for their benefits, because they and not Daisy or Ruth understand their pains. Unlike Daisy and Ruth, the rural women understand the cultural reality of the relationship between male and female but only seek mutual respect and recognition of their power. The women of *Idu* in the play consider themselves jewels and essential actors in nation building and thereby powerful enough to seek freedom but not compete for equality. To Sheriffat, the reality is that:

> We see the world in circles: the male is male, and the female, female.
> No one can take the place of another; nor is one greater than the other.
> Their value is not measured in terms of greater or lesser value.

Each one is priceless in the order of things.
Each one is a part of the other; male and female. It is not a matter of male or female (p. 21).

It is important to note that the acceptance of this position by rural women does not suggest complacency; it is only an ideological difference from the urban women craving radical independence from male domination. The rural women project their pride as mothers and custodians of the kitchen and stomach. Hence, the relationship between men and women has been from inception more complimentary than competitive. Therefore, if women can be educated, they can collectively move mountains and use their managerial expertise to develop our society positively.

Conclusion

Tess Onwueme in *Reign of Wazobia* and *Go tell it to Women* displays a committed quest to re-order the old order of traditional, social, and economic oppression against women folk with modesty. This comes with the hope of reconstructing a new society where mutual respect to human feelings and personage will reign, with the focus of the plays beyond the pedestal calling for gender equality. In fact, Nwachukwu-Agbada (1992: 467) once describes the social change missions of Tess Onwueme dramaturgy in "her quest for social change" as going "beyond the raising of feminist consciousness in society to include a swipe at the diminishing status of supposedly independent African countries because of the powerful gains of neocolonialism".

It is imminent in the end that Onwueme's dramatic adventures mirror her sociological intention to change the status quo by exposing and ridiculing of the obnoxious tradition which limit the political and economic relation between and among gender classes. Onwueme's plays serve to "illuminate the courage of

43

women" in the process of nation building (Azunwo and Omovwiomo, 2015: 7).

It is therefore suggested by the plays that different groups of women, in the political, social, cultural and religious institutions should, as a matter of importance, close ranks, and refocus the drive for elevation of women. This can be achieved with house to house sensitisation, including weekly or quarterly town-gown meetings where the rural women will not only be enlightened about the evils of male hegemony but equally allow them to willingly, like Omu in *Reign...*, see why they must support the course of woman empowerment in the larger scale of society.

REFERENCES

Akinwale, A. (2011). "Joke Silva/Jacob: Live on stage and television", in Salami-Agunloye, I. (ed.), *African women, drama and performance*, Boston: Evergreen Books, pp. 291-296.

Azunwo, E. E. and Omovwiomo, K. O. (2015). "Female dramatists, distinction and the Nigerian society: An examination of Zulu Sofola and Tess Onwueme's selected plays", *Mgbakoigba: Journal of African Studies*. 4: 1-18.

Evwierhoma, M. (2002). *Female empowerment and dramatic creativity in Nigeria*. Ibadan: Caltop Publishers Nigeria Limited.

Ezeigbo, A. (1996). *Gender issues in Nigeria: A feminist perspective*. Lagos: Vista books.

Idegu, E. U. (2009). "Historical overview, global outlook, topical relevance and applicability of feminism", in Idegu, E.U. (ed.)., *Aesthetics and dramaturgy of Irene Salami-Agunloye*, Jos: Department of Theatre and Film Arts, pp. 73-87.

Johnson, S. (1921; 1960 rpt.), *The History of the Yorubas from the Earliest Times to the Beginning of the British Protectorate*, Lagos: CMS (Nigeria) Bookshops, pp. 155-156.

Nwachukwu-Agbada, J. O. J. (1992). *Tess Onwueme: Dramatist in quest of change.* http://www.jstor.org/stable/40148371 (Retrieved on 25 August 2017).

Obadiegwu, C.C. (2009). "From alternative ideology to theoretical diversities: African women rights advocates and the politics of feminism", in Idegu, E.U. (ed.)., *Aesthetics and dramaturgy of Irene Salami-Agunloye*, Jos: Department of Theatre and Film Arts, pp. 88-113.

Ojediran, O. (2011). "Gender talk or powerless female: Efua T. Sutherland's *Edufa* and the M*arriage of Anansewa* as paradigms", *West African Theatre and Performing Arts Journal* (WATPAJO), pp. 37-49.

Onwueme, T. (1992). *The reign of Wazobia and other plays.* Ibadan: Heinemann Educational Books Plc.

Onwueme, T. (1992). *Go tell it to Women.* Newark: African Heritage Press.

Sotunsa, M. (2008). *Feminism and gender discourse: The African experience.* Ogun: Asaba Publications.

THE DRAMATURGY OF RADICAL CONSCIENTISATION IN IRENE SALAMI'S *EMOTAN* AND *IDIA: THE WARRIOR QUEEN*

By Lauretta IKE

Introduction

Feminism as a social movement involves diverse but similar transformational ideologies that resist socio-cultural practices which border on the infringement of freedom and fundamental human rights of the female gender class in the society. It confronts gender oppression, exploitation, discrimination and subjugation in all shades; mostly warranted by several unauthored perhaps obnoxious cultural practices against females by males. Gender has been the defining factor at all ages including the present age and it remains a cardinal element of our humanity. Consequently, it has been the main thrust of most feminist theories over time to attack, expose and proffer strategies for women's liberation from the shackle of patriarchal system. According to Ogundipe (2002: 37), "women are powerless on the basis of the principles of social stratification, which operate in Nigeria". To Ogundipe, women in general lack power, prestige and property.

The enhancement of women's rights and empowerment would require an assessment of all cultural practices in the form of laws and customs that subject women to oppressive and dehumanising practices such as widowhood rites, child marriage, child molestation, child abuse and girls becoming domestic assistants. Consequently, Westernisation and colonialism has robbed women of their right and worth. "The consequence of this is that women are economically marginalised and politically ostracised" (McDonnell, 2003: 21).

The male significance from the corpus of texts and plays renders a terrible threat to the creative prowess of the female factor. This chapter therefore seeks to point out the realities of female activism and power, especially in Africa while dwelling on critics such as Mabel Evwierhoma (2002), Akachi Ezeigbo (1996), Julie Okoh (2000), and Omolara Ogundipe-Leslie (1994) with their assertive zeal in condemning the ignoble and shabby roles of women as portrayed in the creative works by the male writers in the treatment of female characters.

Essentially, this study is an assessment of the innate power of the African woman, her place, role and image in the society. This is because in the belief of Olajubu (2003: 643), "women wield considerable powers with extensive influence. This power is real and potent and yet, is invisible, and cannot be analysed by physical sense".

Within the context of Salami-Agunloye's dramaturgy, the two play texts, *Emotan* and her magnum opus, *Idia: The Warrior Queen of Benin*, expunge male dominance of women. Radical feminism, which is the focus of her theatre, is used to point out the situations that discourage women from seeking formal and informal positions in a patriarchal society. In these plays, she articulates the need for change. In fact, her plays are "an analysis of woman's subordination for the purpose of figuring out how to change it" (Moh, 2005: 33). The playwright fashions her artistic gong to answer the following questions:

- Are women economically viable?
- Are they active within the confines of their family and in the society?

- Have they the willpower to unwind the stigmatisation placed on them by patriarchy?

In response to the questions, and since theatre is one avenue for appropriating artistic and intellectual development, this chapter examines the playwright's radical, positive and noble quests for feminine consciousness and the evolving power base to challenge gender consciousness in our society. It further highlights the unhealthy cultural, traditional and societal milieu conditioning the feminine gender existence and survival, bringing out the critical focus of feminine struggle for valid recognition as envisioned in the two plays.

Literature Review: A Conceptual Clarification

Feminism is an ideology embraced by writers, dramatists, social activists and playwrights such as Julie Okoh, Tess Onwueme, Mabel Evwierhoma, Zulu Sofola, Oludolapo Ojediran, Irene Salami-Agunloye, Omolara Ogundipe-Leslie and Osita Ezenwanebe who have, through their creative works, articulated views to correct the misrepresentation of females. All these are dramatists, literary icons and female social activists.

As a conscious effort, feminism is aimed at a criticism of women inferiorization – their role, character, image and essence. It became an organized movement in the 19th century, as people increasingly came to believe that women were being treated unfairly with emphasis on the physical and psychological differences between women and men. This is very glaring in the submission of Ezeigbo (1996: 1) that "feminism is ideologically designed to liberate and emancipate women worldwide from oppression, ignorance, poverty and self-immolation". As in most traditional societies, women have been undervalued more than men, and more often marginalised and relegated for socio-cultural reasons.

The earliest form of feminism is concerned with equal rights for women and men. This meant equal standing as citizens in public life and to some extent, equal legal status within the home. Feminism means different things to different people. Nonetheless, it is an increasing sensitivity to the inequalities of sexism.

> As an ideology, feminism smacks of rebelliousness, fearlessness, political awareness of sexism, and an unpardonable drive (from the male point of view) for equality and equity between the sexes. It therefore instils fear in men though it thrills many women (Ogunbiyi, 1988: 65).

Also, Ojediran (2012: 44) confirms that:

> Although feminism has produced a range of theoretical frameworks from which women's roles and personality in society are explored with the aim of developing a better understanding of the conditions that underwrite power relationships between men and women across different societies, it would be erroneous to say that all sex difference in language are aimed at creating female stereotypes and insults to the female gender.

By the turn of the century, women rights movements emerged in part from women's sense of alliance with one another and their shared discontents. In Africa, women play crucial roles in the economic and social sectors of their economies. The analysis of this fact is summed up by Morolake Omonubi-McDonnell (2003: 10), "one thing that women in Africa have in common is the undisputed fact that they are the pillars of production and the bedrock of the family; generalising them as a lump of subordinates is a misplacement of fact". Over time, several sub-types of feminist ideology have developed in the light of radical feminism, liberal feminism, cultural feminism, black feminism, socialist feminism and so on.

Radical Feminism: It is the breeding ground for many of the ideas arising from feminism. Radical feminism questions why women must adopt certain roles based on their biology, just as it questions why men adopt certain other roles based on theirs. Radical feminism views the oppression of women as fundamental and more diabolical than other forms of injustice in the society.

Liberal Feminism: This variety of feminism asserts the equality of men and women through political and legal reform. It is an individualistic form of feminism that focuses on women's ability to integrate into the society's structure and use the available processes to achieve compromises, and to transform the society.

Cultural Feminism: This type stipulates that there are fundamental personality differences between men and women and that women's differences and should be specially celebrated. This came into existence as radical feminism dies out as a movement. In fact, many of the same people moved from liberal feminism to radical feminism. A striking difference in the two is that radical feminism was out to transform society while cultural feminism was working towards building women's culture in the society
(http://www.encarta.msn.com/encyclopedia/feminism.html; retrieved on 20 September 2017).

Black Feminism: This movement is mainly upheld by black and cultural feminists. They condemn their white feminist counterparts for racial and colour discrimination. Evwierhoma (2002: 44) explains that, "black feminism emerged after the early feminist movements that were led specifically by white women who advocated social changes such as women's suffrage". To this, she further maintains that, "the womanist under this theory seek a reassessment of the woman of African descent in society through the contemporary reality she faces" (2002: 45).

Socialist Feminism: Marxism recognises that women are oppressed and attributes this to the capitalist system. Thus, they insist that the only way to end the oppression of women is to overthrow the capitalist system. Evwierhoma (2002: 43) offers a description of socialist feminism as "the belief that male or patriarchal ideas are dominant in the society and female ideas are subordinated to them because they control production". Adherents of this movement see the need to work alongside not just men, but all other groups, as they see the oppression of women as a part of a larger pattern that affects everyone involved in the capitalist system.

Synopsis of the Selected Plays

Emotan is a historical play that revolves around the eponymous character Emotan who helps Prince Okoro Ogun, also known as Ewuare the Great, ascend the throne of Benin kingdom. Displeased at the way the kingmakers plotted and sent Ogun on exile and aided Oba Uwaifiokun to usurp the throne of Benin, Emotan vows to help Ogun regain the kingship of Benin. In the play, she typifies a woman's role in the home-front, outside the home and in the means of production and ownership of capital.

Emotan raises a secret army to conscientize the people towards agitating for Okoro Ogun's return from exile and enthronement. She would sneak around town during the day gathering information from the wives and children of the kingmakers and feed Ogun with this information. She equally renders uncommon assistance to her gender at that time. She assists Ogun's return from exile as king, upon which Ogun banishes the usurper Uwaifiokun.

Idia: The Warrior Queen of Benin speaks a lot of women's status in African society. The play dramatizes the pains and gains of women in nation building, as well as the struggle between tradition and change. Irene Salami-Agunloye is so disheartened that many millennia into the existence of mankind, women are yet to be given their proper place of pride in the society. The play centres on a dominant female character, Idia, who seeks to correct the obnoxious custom of Benin that enforces the death of a Queen Mother upon ascendance of her son to the throne. Idia worries over this tradition which she calls a 'wasteful one' and resolves to stop the killing of Queen Mothers.

In disagreeing with the tradition of killing Queen Mothers according to tradition, a group of protesting market women led by Sogie, Idia's friend, demand a compromise from the Oba, and succeed. Sogie demands that no Queen Mother loses her life because of her son's ascension to the throne of Benin. The playwright in a way challenges patriarchal structures and the oppressive cultural practices that have affected the female characters in the play. The playwright however mirrors the conflicting and complex nature of intra-gender and inter-gender relationship instances in our society.

Character Constructs and Voice of Change in the Plays

Emotan and *Idia: The Warrior Queen of Benin* are voice constructions on change. With these plays, the playwright canvasses for change in the social order. She questions why women must adopt certain roles based on the biology of the woman. For instance, Idia in *Idia: The Warrior Queen of Benin* courageously opposes the tradition that upholds the slaying of the mother of the reigning king. Idia challenges and tells her friends thus:

> **Idia**: It is time to stop this wasteful tradition. A waterpot that is no longer useful must be discarded. A gossip that has been said over and over again becomes a pain to the ear. Enough is enough (*Idia*, p. 4).

This tradition of the king's mother as a ritual scapegoat for the fortune of her son, is one of the few injustices meted on women. In most traditional African societies, women are accepted as objects of rituals. In the olden times especially in Urhobo society, a neighbouring community to Benin, maidens (especially virgins) were sacrificed to appease the gods. The potency of such sacrifices is believed to assure bountiful harvest, abundant rainfall and so on. With Idia's statement, Iyiesogie becomes conscious of Idia's position on the ritual scapegoatism. She succumbs to Idia's radical opinion for change. Iyiesogie hence accepts a new and different approach which contradicts the existing laws, customs and norms. Furthermore, Oba Esigie, an ardent propagator of tradition later conforms to Idia's point of view about human sacrifice. In fact, he symbolises the male feminist who supports the women's empowerment forum. His views are not in consonance with his chiefs who behave as cultural nationalists. Binebai (2015: 208) notes that:

For the privileged class who must speak for the subaltern, there is the need for the fulfilment of an ethical task; the task of establishing a strong and positive moral relationship with those at the margins. This is the only way occupiers of privileged positions can speak for the subaltern subject. Spivak is therefore of the view that there must be an interaction between privileged class and the subaltern subject to ennoble and enable subaltern representation by the privileged class.

Oba Esigie is one of the privileged who speaks for the subaltern. His task of obliterating the barbaric tradition of the sacrifice of a woman must be fulfilled. With *Idia: The Warrior Queen of Benin*, Irene Salami-Agunloye speaks for the subjugated and marginalised women the world over. The character Idia articulates that the time has come for change to take its course. This is the time for women to proclaim their liberty, as well as empowerment for the female gender.

In *Emotan* for instance, the playwright depicts the nature of women in Benin society, and the world in a larger framework. The rich tradition of Benin land ostracises women from salient activities in the societies. In fact, its tradition sometimes sees women as object of sacrifice. Irene Salami-Agunloye uses her works to express her disheartenment that for many millennia, women are challenged, side lined and yet to be given their proper place of pride in the workforce. This mirrors the political situation in Nigeria and Africa where men are seen as the big wigs in the political structure. Women are not considered for major political appointments. Major political cadres are the birth right of men. Hence, using *Emotan*, Irene Salami-Agunloye sensitises the society while reflecting on the hope and dilemma that follows the feminine gender. Like Aristophanes' play *Lysistrata*, Emotan and Idia play a major role in the leadership structure of their community. They resolve to deal with the issues of women subjugation, calling for women to stand up for themselves and improve their lot. Thus, the playwright insists that women should not accept demeaning conditions simply because they find themselves in it. The female characters in these plays fall under these categories – powerful, weak but strong, influential, resourceful and useful.

The heroic characters in both plays unearth some of the reasons behind feminine agitations. These agitations are geared towards fighting for their rights and refuting negative practices, which has become entrenched over time in our cultures. They grow headstrong to battle and free themselves from the shackles society has placed on them over the centuries. The plays reveal a reflection of the playwright's responsibility in affirming a woman's strong impact on her society. That Salami-Agunloye writes on women in politics buttresses the opinion of Ogundipe-Leslie (1994: 208) that "African women must still organize and confront the problems of gender in their own cultures".

In confronting the problems of gender in her culture, Salami-Agunloye did not align herself with the conventional issues of marriage, immorality, childbirth, love and infidelity. She captures vividly the essential aspect of her culture that expresses her inherent ideological stance as the plays speak volume of the centrality of the African woman in many of our social platforms.

From the foregoing, we shall therefore assess the playwright's radical ideology, philosophy and ideas that pervade our chosen plays.

The Dramaturgy of Radical Conscientization in the Plays

Evident in the two plays are ideas about female empowerment, gender disparity and the need for equality in inter-gender power relations. There is an attempt to use the plays as tools of communication at generating valid and positive responses towards the improvement of the plight of womanhood and furtherance of progress in our societies. We see a reflection of the beauty of the African woman in its different manifestations. The plays equally point to the history of African culture with emphasis on the female prowess in decision making over matters affecting the community.

Salami-Agunloye uses her two plays to portray the independent will of women to fight, agitate, negotiate and survive against the status quo economic, political and socio-cultural limitation in the society. Rejecting the dogmatic belief about traditions, Salami-Agunloye in *Idia: The Warrior Queen of Benin* exposes the negative effect of obnoxious traditions in the progress of our society:

> **Idia**: No Iyesogie, for a long time, I thought so too, I used to believe that tradition was unchangeable but now I think you are wrong. Tradition does not dictate the pace of our individual or national progress; we are to determine that (p. 3).

What is important here is that her treatment of the women issues cannot be taken to stand for the way other women writers treat these same issues. To a large extent, the plot of *Idia: The Warrior Queen of Benin* dwells on the periodic dialectics of culture and its dynamism. It projects the richness of our cultural heritage in proverbial discourses in a normal African traditional society.

The first act in *Emotan* reveals the celebrative mood of the village women on their festive day. Meanwhile, Emotan is emotionally withdrawn amidst the women. She is sad, quiet and refuses to give up her leaf as expected. From this moment on, she is established as pursuing an extreme and radical female consciousness with the mission to uncover some extreme harmful traditional practices. By implication, this means that to some degree the female persona can stand up to her right in refusing segregation, violence, intimidation and insubordination. And when it comes to governing affairs, they can equally reject the harem of a usurper, a traitor and a schemer as it is better emphasised in the play.

The playwright tries to strike a balance in the radical character of Emotan with that of other female characters like Imose, Iriowen, Eki and Imade. These characters are created to spite the effort of Emotan thereby posing a challenge, which further gingers and enables her to achieve the noble course of liberation. This is pointing to the fact that one in a million of radical feminists not only comes in opposition with the opposite sex but with the same sex as it is portrayed in the busy-bodied and nonchalant attitudes of these minor female characters. However, the play emphasises that partnership, collaboration and negotiation should be advocated for in national development. This is what Tobrise (1993: 104) tags "the ideology of revolt in Nigerian feminist theatre" in her paper, *The Ideology of Revolt in Nigerian Feminist Theatre: The Wives Revolt and the Rebellion of the Bumpy Chested*. Tobrise examines and situates J.P Clark's *The Wives Revolt* and Stella Oyedepo's *Rebellion of the Bumpy Chested* in the repertoire of radical feminism.

Salami-Agunloye in a telephone conversation in 2009 with this author appropriates the position of radical feminists as she notes that:

> Those concerned here don't have regards for men and they are the ones that say a woman should not bear MRS. They preach a separate world for women. They try to rewrite language in such a way that it becomes gender-neutral e.g. the use of human kind instead of mankind.

An analysis of the above is captured in the play when Idia addresses Ologbose:

> **Idia**: Go ahead, train and re-train them for battle. There is no going back. Chief Oliha has thrown us a challenge; he has openly declared war. We have no alternative but to respond (p. 66).

She is quite radical in her attempt to fight at the war front, a task commonly taken up by men. She enjoys a great deal of autonomy in her exercise of right as the Queen Mother. In the acts that run towards the end of the play, Idia displays authority in decision making, taking up leadership roles. She is determined to do so against Chief Oliha's challenge.

> **Idia**: Then I will fight the battle. You have challenged me and I will rise up to the challenge. I am going to mobilize the warriors for battle myself, fight the battle and return home victorious. (p. 73).

Chief Oliha challenges Idia to a war, turning against everyone in the Kingdom including the Oba. Sensing his frustrated state of mind, she sends him two beautiful ladies to replace his lost wives. But he turns violent chasing them away and screaming at

58

the top of his voice, *"War! War!! War!!!"* (p. 64). Courageously, Idia responds in like-mind shouting, *"War? War then it must be"* (p. 65).

As radical as this may seem, the playwright presents a determined woman, an empowered feminine gender who enacts strength, confidence, vigour, poise and power in the focus of their freedom, rather than remaining conservative, inactive and silent in the face of mockery, opposition and challenge. We can see this in the derogatory statements by Iyase and Ihama as stated below:

> **Ihama**: Your Majesty, I must remind you that although the butterfly imitates the bird, it can never be a bird. This battle is not for women.
>
> **Iyase**: Why do you want to get involved in everything in this Kingdom? Do you know that you are a woman? You will soon realize that he who dances to every music will soon be lame on both legs (pp. 73 -74).

Radical feminism is one approach used in these plays to point out the disagreeing factor in male domination over the female. Salami-Agunloye is out to expose some features in the traditional set up that works towards the subordination of women. Within the context of the plays, she dwells on radicalism as a relevant cause to feminine limited autonomy. Radicalism is simply being different from others in opinions, ideas, views and actions. If feminism can be said to be "an analysis of woman's subordination for the purpose of figuring out how to change it" (Moh, 2005: 33), then Salami-Agunloye, through these plays, projects women who are clamouring for revolution and emancipation in a masculinist society. The saying that "what a man can do a woman can do better is replete in media as a reality and only reinforce the belief that all man does is good thus inadvertently glorifying masculinity by imitating it" (Oyewo, 2012: 140).

An analysis of these plays reveals a rooted understanding of the conceptual status of womanhood, the context of women's complementary and inevitable choice in canvassing for change and social order. To further expound this, we observe that the playwright achieves a thorough picture of the character, Idia in *Idia: The Warrior Queen of Benin* when she opposes the tradition that upholds the slaying of the Mother of the reigning King.

> **Idia**: It is time to stop this wasteful tradition. A waterpot that is no longer useful must be discarded. A gossip that has been said over and over again becomes a pain to the ear. Enough is enough! (p. 4)

The play *Emotan* is starkly within a referential point. In the opening scene, the character of Emotan is among the group of women who notably celebrates the Ewere festival seasonally. The carrying of the Ewere leaves and their harmonised singing symbolises peace and tranquillity in the community. But where a member stands out in a depressed state of mind, mood and action, where is the place of communal peace and tranquillity? Even when Iriowen, the women leader collects their Ewere leaves, Emotan refuses to give up hers. She is withdrawn, sad and quiet. Her radicalism has shown from the onset in her attitude, even where spoken words elude her.

All of these were not unnoticed as Uwaifiokun, the Oba, called the attention of the chiefs who are present. They all know obviously that her reaction is tailored towards the injustice meted out on Prince Ogun, the apparent heir to the throne. In his ploy to deal with her, the Oba sends his men to bring her to his harem and make her one of his wives. This causes a very blunt disapproval by Emotan, and her attitude confirms to that of a radical who will simply not succumb to insubordination. The lines below sum it up:

> **Emotan**: Tell him I have never taken delight in being a queen and I never will. I am content with my present status. Tell the Oba to stay in his place and enjoy the company of his numerous queens. Thank you (p. 30).

Salami-Agunloye applies most of the views and aspirations of the female characters in *Idia: The Warrior Queen of Benin* to *Emotan*. Here, we find similar situations woven around their aim at creating a common forum for women's struggle for their emancipation. Even when armed men are in guard in the forest where Prince Ogun remains in exile, Emotan still finds a way to sneak out daily to feed him with both food and information on her various strategic attempts at freeing him.

The playwright chooses female characters to tactically stir a whole warrior camp, and at the end a successful mission is achieved. It is revealed in Emotan's speech on page 55 that the women are marching naked to the palace the next day in protest of the injustice done to Prince Ogun. If "the greatest strength of women lies their right and ability to work in addition to their resourcefulness and great capacity for survival" according to Ogundipe-Leslie (1994: 77), then in relation to this play *Emotan*, we can find it quite amazing that a woman can accept a sacrifice of her own life to save another. Thus:

Okutukutu: You are the only sacrifice that can bring Okoro Ogun to his throne and peace to Benin. There is no other person we can offer (p. 63).

Her response to the diviner signifies the greatest display of a woman's emotional strength in the face of great challenge:

Emotan: O wicked and treacherous world. What can I do now? What choice do I have? I have always lived my life for humanity, for Benin and for Ogun. Difficult though it may be, I have no choice. I have gone too far to back out. This is a costly sacrifice indeed. I am ready to pay the price (p. 64).

This act calls for a gradual change in the belief that women can't contribute immensely to national development and be ably represented politically if given the chance. Thus, this is seen to be the peak of radicalism being emphasised by the playwright in her prolific and vision to actualise women empowerment in the society.

Critical Perspectives

In a sense, Salami-Agunloye uses the plays to mirror the exceptional challenges facing African and contemporary Nigerian women. According to Evwierhoma (2002: 121), "writers must align themselves with the people, in their struggle for freedom and quest for a new society". This can be deduced easily from the successful victory of both heroines in the plays under our study, in relation to the end where the result of their actions manifests in jubilation; invariably, the society is pleased with their victorious feats.

What is considered good, normal and desirable are mostly associated with a patriarchal society. Under the guise of custom, patriarchy sets some standards, practices and demands for compliance among the members of a given society. Preventing the set standards and norms of behaviour as conditions for inhabitants to belong in a given society pre-occupies the theme of these plays in our analysis.

In her painstaking dramaturgy and creative writing style, the playwright exhibits the continuous struggle of women with stereotype that can prove to be serious obstacle in attaining certain leadership cadre, achieving development goals and careers in their community. The language in the two plays proves remarkable in that it portrays the platform for an in-depth understanding of feminine leadership legacy which must be sustained. The dominant perspectives perpetuate values for emulation in women, stimulating in them vitality, creativity and courage for sustainable social change. This further exposes them to the world they live in, encourages and awakens their intelligence in questioning the system that limits their lives and choices.

The truth of art is therefore mediated by the playwright's vision as expressed by Ogundipe-Leslie, thus pointing to Salami-Agunloye as an artist and a visionary who presents the truth of her culture surrounding the situation of women in present day Nigeria, as well as proffering a better society in the future if women's value is considered and appreciated.

There is need therefore for writers to treat positions of women in the society truthfully without dwelling on only the traditional fixed roles that the society tags them with – child bearers, kitchen managers, bedroom warmers and the likes. Plays on feminine issues should bring up ideological points of view that uphold and reflect contemporary issues that meaningfully portray womanhood in the light of socio-political cum political activism, beyond the *other room*[1].

Conclusion

The two plays are premised on the concept of female empowerment, gender disparity and, most importantly, they speak for the maligned women in the society to be conscious of the need for a change in this social status quo. The plays also function as tools of generating valid and positive responses towards the improvement and progress of our societies with the involvement of women. The plays further expatiate on female prowess in matters affecting the community. In a dramatic context, female characters are clearly the representation of the feminine presence in a patriarchal society. Irene Salami-Agunloye thus represents a paradigm of creative writers who speak against oppression, suppression, domination and subjugation by the phallic hegemony of the male gender.

One fundamental pre-occupation of this study has been to analyse two selected plays of Salami-Agunloye, *Emotan* and *Idia: The warrior queen of Benin*. In the play texts, she has chosen to treat women in a more reformative and revolutionary way using her as compared to the way other writers address their issues. She asserts, in a phone conversation in 2009, that "what women are denied of is what they most fight for. I try to bring out the picture of the struggling woman towards redeeming her from her inferior status". Therefore, that women should seek collaboration with the men in the manifestation of growth, peaceful co-existence and development in the society.

---

[1] Derogatory reference to the bedroom as the other place for women, apart from the kitchen.

REFERENCES

Binebai, B. (2015). "Voice construction in the postcolonial text: Spivakian subaltern theory in Nigerian drama", in *An International Multidisciplinary Journal, Ethiopia* Vol. 9(4), pp. 206-220.

Evwierhoma, M. (2002). *Female empowerment and dramatic creativity in Nigeria*. Ibadan: Caltop Publishers Nigeria Limited.

Ezeigbo, T. A. (1996). *Gender issues in Nigeria: A feminine perspective*. Lagos: Vista Books Limited, Nigeria.

Moh, F. A. (2005). *Women in literature: Selected plays*. Port Harcourt: Amethyst and Colleagues Publishers.

Ogunbiyi, Y. (1988). *Perspectives in Nigerian literature: 1700 to present*. Lagos: Guardian Books Nigeria Limited, Nigeria.

Ogundipe, A. (2002). "Power in gender discourse", in Ukhun C. E. (Ed.) *Critical Gender discourse in Africa*, Ibadan: Hope Publications, pp. 31-43.

Ogundipe-Leslie, M. (1994). *Recreating ourselves: African women and critical transformations*. New Jersey: African World Press, Inc.

Ojediran, O. (2012). *Speaking in an alien voice: A womanist comparison of the use of language by Scottish and West African female playwrights*. A Ph.D. Thesis Submitted to Queen Margaret University, Edinburgh.

Okoh, J. (2000). *In the fullness of time*. Owerri: Total Publishers.

Olajubu, O. (2003). "Women and power structure in Africa", in Dopamu A. P. (Ed.) *African culture, modern science and religious thought*, Ilorin: African Centre for Religions and the Sciences (ACRS), pp. 642-651.

Omonubi-McDonnell, M. (2003). *Gender inequality in Nigeria.* Ibadan: Spectrum Books Limited.

Oyewo, S. (2012). "Gender in African theatre: A discourse of female aesthetics in Nigerian theatre", in *West African Theatre and Performing Arts Journal,* 1(2); pp. 130-143.

Salami-Agunloye, I. (2008). *Idia, the Warrior Queen of Benin.* Jos: Saniez Publications.

Salami, I. (2001). *Emotan (A Benin Heroine).* Jos: Mazlink Nigeria Limited.

Tobrise, M. (1993). "The Ideology of Revolt in Nigerian Feminist Theatre: *The Wives Revolt* and the *Rebellion of the Bumpy Chested*", in J. Malomo and S. Gbilekaa (eds.), *Theatre and politics in Nigeria,* Ibadan: Caltop Publications, pp. 104 - 115.

INTERVIEWS

Salami-Agunloye, I., telephone interview with Lauretta Ike, on 9 June 2009.

DRAMATIC REALISATIONS IN LANGUAGE, CULTURE AND COMMON GROUND IN IRENE ISOKEN SALAMI'S *EMOTAN*

Oluwatomi ADEOTI

Introduction

Language is an intrinsic part of a people's culture and it defines their very essence. Indeed, a people's use of language transcends its employment towards a communicative end; it is a part of their culture and a form of identity. This position reflects the importance of language to individuals and on a larger scale, to a community of people. A people's culture which accounts for their beliefs, ideologies and general outlook for life is the backdrop against which communities are built and their actions and inactions established. It is therefore common to hear expressions like a "culture of waste", a culture of corruption, or a culture of hard work and dedication, when references are made to particular people, groups or countries. The implication of this is that individuals or groups of people are judged by their culture and their disposition to life. Consequently, individuals belonging to the same linguistic, professional, cultural or religious community can be said to share a culture which defines. Such shared understanding, background and experience has been dubbed Common Ground by language scholars.

Various accounts of Common Ground (CG) have been presented by several scholars, including Lewis, 1979; Stalnaker, 1978; Clark, 1996, 2006; Horton, 2008; Enfield, 2008; Kecskes, 2014. Some of these scholars posit that CG is the totality of the information available to interlocutors which is considered key for a smooth communicative endeavour during an interaction. Others believe though CG makes for better and more effective communication, given the capability of information sharing that is available to both the speaker and hearer at the time of the conversation, such information, in the event that it is not available, can be accessed in the form of emergent CG (Kecskes, 2014). Such information can be supplied and accommodated during the conversation.

Enfield (2008) posits that CG is a resource that speakers exploit in inviting and deriving pragmatic inference, consequently cutting costs of speech production by relying on the shared information available to both the speakers and hearers, and invariably the inferencing ability of the listeners. Common Ground is "indispensable for philosophical and cognitive conceptions of knowledge where it serves as background for reasoning and for retrieving speaker-intended meaning and other types of implicit meaning, such as indexical expression or implicature" (Fetzer, 2011: 33). This background for reasoning and uncovering the communicative intention of the speaker requires requisite knowledge of the cultural orientations, religious beliefs, socio-political realities and ideological inclinations of the speaker. The assertion that every writer or speaker is a product of his or her environment and their perceptions to life and their writings or speech is thus informed.

The position explained above is echoed in Babatunde (2007: 182) when he observes that "...the socio-cultural awareness, the degree to which he (a writer) is rooted in his environment is largely manifested in the way these relevant linguistic and contextual features flow wittingly or otherwise into his writing". The writers' awareness of the socio-cultural beliefs is important in the encoding of the message and the ultimate interpretation by the reader. This is a function of the provisions of the common ground shared by the cartoonist and the readers (Adeoti, 2015: 6). This chapter is premised on how these provisions of culture, shared experiences, whether based on experiential knowledge or knowledge informed by being co-users of a language, interact to unequivocally communicate the intentions of the playwright in the context of the play and in the wider context of the society. It examines the representation and instances of CG in Irene Salami-Agunloye's *Emotan* with a view to establishing how she constructs the play text. Further, it considers the social, political and ideological underpinnings of the society where the play is set and how these are represented in the use of language as well as based on her communicative intentions.

Theoretical Considerations

Communication is said to thrive on the amount of shared information that is available to interlocutors before and during conversations (Wheelwright, 1975; Stalnaker, 1978; Bach & Harnish, 1979; Santon, 2004). Such shared information is termed contextual beliefs. Bach & Harnish (1979) in particular refer to it as Mutual Contextual Beliefs (MCBs). They opine that "the inference made by the hearer and the inference he takes himself to be intended to make is based, not just on what the speaker says but also on mutual contextual beliefs (MCBs)" (1979: 5). The apparent MCBs in the speaker's intentions and the hearer's inference must, consequently, be mutual for successful communication. MCBs can therefore be represented as being a part of the Common Ground of Interlocutors. Several scholars have presented various accounts of Common Ground (CG), including Lewis, 1979; Stalnaker, 1978; Clark, 1996, 2006; Horton, 2008; Enfield, 2008; and Kecskes, 2014. A summation of their propositions is that CG is the totality of the information which is considered key for a smooth communicative endeavour available to interlocutors during an interaction. This CG can however be accessed in the form of emergent CG (Kecskes, 2014), as such information can be supplied and accommodated during the conversation, if the information is not available prior to any point of the conversation.

Clark (1996: 92) posits that "everything we do is rooted in information about our surrounding, activities, perceptions, interests, etc. Everything we do jointly with others is also rooted in this information, but only in that part we think they share with us". Common Ground is thus a prerequisite for everything we do with others. To interact effectively therefore, interlocutors need to keep track of their Common Ground as it accumulates incrementally. Irene Isoken Salami exhibits this reliance on CG as she, in the play text *Emotan* leaves out certain information, taking for granted that it constitutes a part of the shared knowledge, either in the context of the text or the context in the text. This is an exemplification of Stalnaker's (1978, 2002) submission on CG. He explains that in interaction, people presuppose certain things and what is presupposed guides what they choose to say and how they intend what they say to be interpreted. By this, Stalnaker presents the idea of Common Ground based on presupposition. Explaining that to "presuppose something is to take it for granted, or at least to act as if one takes it for granted, as background information – as *common ground* among the participants in the conversation" (Stalnaker, 2002: 701), Stalnaker accounts for common ground as a social or public attitude because a speaker presupposes ϕ only if he/she presupposes that others presuppose it as well.

Clark (2009: 116) defines Common Ground as "the sum of the information that people assume they share" and identifies two sources of Common Ground: Common ground based on community membership (communal common ground) and common ground based on personal experience. Communal Common Ground is information common to a group or community of people, which can, for example, be a community of shared culture, practices or expertise, e.g. a 'community' of lawyers or Nigerians. Members of such communities display their communal identities in their choice of language, dressings, and mannerisms among others (Clark, 2006). The content of communal common ground includes: communal lexicon, cultural facts, norms and procedures, ineffable background, graded information, ideologies and socio-cultural doxa among others. Personal Common Ground on the other hand, is based on joint experience and may be perceptual, linguistic or communicative.

Enfield (2008: 225) defines Common Ground to be "a resource that speakers exploit in inviting and deriving pragmatic inference, as a way to cut costs of speech production by leaving much to be inferred by the listener". In explaining how mutual knowledge and beliefs are accessed, Enfield identifies three sources of Common Ground: joint attention, shared experiential knowledge and shared cultural knowledge. Joint attention refers to a situation where both speakers are aware of the presence of an entity in the discourse space and simultaneously attend to that external stimulus, with each of them conscious that the experience is shared. This is an example of 'physical co-presence'.

Shared experiential knowledge pertains to experiences that the discourse participants know and remember that is shared. At the cultural level, Common Ground may be indexed by signs of ethnic identity and the common cultural background that such signs may entail e.g. native dialect signalled by accent (Enfield, 2008: 224). He asserts that this will lead to other assumptions of

71

Common Ground. Furthermore, Enfield submits that Common Ground is of great importance in social and interpersonal relationship. This is because the management of information has social consequences and in interaction, social affiliations in human relationships are managed through the details of communicative practices (Enfield, 2008: 223). Three levels where Common Ground can be indicated include: personal level, cultural level and socio-political level. Common Ground at the personal level is expressed through any shared and remembered joint activity. At the cultural level, common ground is articulated via native dialect, accent, particularised expressions, and established referents. The socio-cultural level involves common ground of current and past events in the community which enjoyed or are enjoying national attention.

Kesckes (2014) posits that commonalities, conventions, common beliefs, shared beliefs and other related concepts create a core common ground which forms a kind of collective salience on which intention and cooperation-based pragmatics is established. Kecskes also submits that sometimes, in conversation, core common ground might be missing or limited, and will therefore need to be co-constituted for the current purpose. Thus, Common Ground should be "created in the interactional context in which the interlocutors function as core common ground creators rather than just common ground seekers or activators..." (2014: 2). Kecskes makes a distinction between three components of common ground, viz, information that the participants share, understanding the situational context and relationships between the participants. Presenting a socio-cognitive approach to the study Common Ground, he emphasises that common ground is a dynamic construct that is mutually constructed by interlocutors throughout the communicative process from prior and emergent elements. Consequently, two sides of common ground are

72

identified: core common ground (which refers to the relatively static, generalised common knowledge and beliefs that usually belong to specific speech communities based on prior interactions and experience) and emergent common ground (which refers to the dynamic, particularised knowledge created – and updated – during communication and triggered by the actual situational context). Though Kecskes' new idea of 'emergent common ground' is more dynamic than existing perspectives of common ground as a static phenomenon, Lewis' (1969) principle of accommodation accounts for such emergent knowledge created during communication as such knowledge is grounded, and subsequently added to the existing common ground

This chapter's consideration of CG in Irene Isoken Salami-Agunloye's *Emotan* is thus premised on this conceptualisation of CG. The reliance on the provisions of CG and how they are expanded in conversations and how they resonate with the cultural underpinnings of the society, inform the ideologies and ultimately further the communicative intentions of play is explored in this paper.

Irene Isoken Salami-Agunloye and *Emotan*

Irene Salami-Agunloye (nee Salami) is a native of Edo State in Nigeria. She is female academic and dramatist whose passion for women and women-related issues is quintessentially reflected in her writings. She is concerned with the actualisation of the full potential of the female and in the process agitates for the abdication of the traditional relegation of women to the kitchen and the background in the home, workplace and political arena of the nation. She challenges women to rise above the bar set by their male counterparts and be active participants in the quest of liberating themselves in their societies. She is a lecturer at the Department of Theatre and Communication Arts, University of

Jos, Nigeria. Irene Salami-Agunloye's creative works include *Emotan* (2001), *The Queen Sisters* (2002), *More than Dancing* (2003), *Sweet Revenge* (2004), and *Idia the Warrior Queen of Benin* (2008).

Emotan is a historical play that celebrates the power of a woman in an oppressive and male dominating culture. It is a play that depicts the stereotypical corner into which the woman has been boxed in the Benin society (the physical setting of the play) and in the general Nigerian cultural setting. The play highlights how a culture "in its richness hemlines women, limiting their autonomy, through taboos and observances which many see as obsolete, behind the times and retrogressive" (Evwierhoma, 2009: 42). Emotan is a loving and simple market woman who encourages the women to be more active in the society by going outside of the confines of their roles in the home. She is representative of a woman who was in charge at home, in her business, and in the matters of the state. Overall, she is portrayed as a self-sufficient woman who does not rely on any man for identity or approval. Emotan displays the strength of a woman, both physically and intellectually as she personally organizes an army to help Ewuare the Great (Ogun) reclaim his throne. Her inner strength is brought to the fore when she commits to pay the ultimate sacrifice for that mission to be realised. *Emotan* can therefore be said to be a play that reiterates the positive image of women for who they really are, outside of the overwhelming shadows of African masculinity, where men are regarded to be the head of the women.

Language, Culture and Common Ground in *Emotan*

Our analysis of the play text shall be based on figure 1 below which is an exemplification of the interaction between language and culture and how they form part of the CG and also show their implications for the success of communicative intention of the play text which, essentially, is to project the woman as an ineligible force in the Benin society primarily and in the nation as a whole.

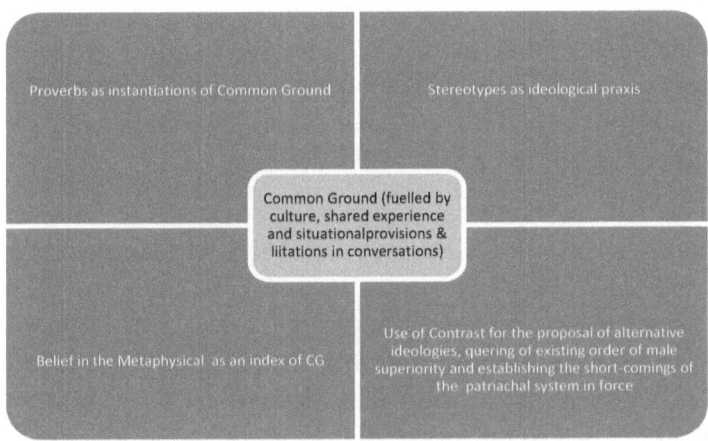

Figure 1: A Model of Language, Culture and Common Ground in *Emotan*

Figure 1 shows the interaction between language and the society which constitutes the people who use the language. Here, CG is at the core of the communicative process as it is fuelled by culture, shared experience and situational provisions and limitations. This accounts for what the society condones in certain situations and frowns at in other situations and also the expectations of language use in the society. Consequently, four major instances of CG as observed *Emotan* include the use of proverbs as instantiations of CG, stereotypes as ideological praxis, belief in the metaphysical as an index of CG and the use of contrast for the proposal of alternative ideologies, querying of the existing order of male superiority and establishing the failings of the patriarchal system in force.

The employment of proverbs indexes the characters' shared cultural experience in the play. The play is replete with instances of the use of proverbs as they serve more functions than mere embellishments. Stereotypes as ideological praxis also demonstrate how women are stereotyped in a bid to typify the womenfolk as being weak, obnoxious and of no consequence in the society. This is also a part of the CG as the belief of the Benin society and the larger society in which the play is set is that the man is superior to the woman.

The African traditional worldview is considered to be a shared phenomenon as it forms a part of the African people's CG. Such aspects of their *weltanschauung* include the belief in the metaphysical and the ancestral. The play text thus makes constant references to terms such as 'the gods', 'ancestors', 'ancestral spirits', which they believe are at the helm of affairs of the things in the physical realm.

Another indication of CG is when *Emotan* employs the use of contrast for the proposal of alternative ideologies, querying of existing order of male superiority and highlighting the shortcomings of the patriarchal system in force. This constitutes a part of the CG as some, if not all, of these issues are a part of the shared social, cultural and political realities of the participants in the play text and in the larger context of the society in which the play text is set. The cultural factors that have informed such standpoints as it relates to the treatment of women as second fiddle in the society are thus accounted for through this index of CG. These are discussed below as they relate to the treatment of women and as examples of attempts at deconstructing the patriarchal ideology in *Emotan*.

Proverbs as Instantiations of Common Ground

The use of proverbs in *Emotan* is considered as an aspect of communal Common Ground (Communal CG). This is because proverbs are a part of a people's culture and their perception of the world can be understood from the use of proverbs. This perhaps informs the high esteem in which proverbs are held by African people who believe that proverbs are more than just mere embellishments of speech; rather, they are of greater value in achieving the communicative intentions of the speakers. They are nuggets of wisdom that provide insights on any thinkable subject of human existence. It is therefore common place to find elders in Nigerian communities communicating their thoughts, feelings and ideas through proverbs which they expect their listeners to be able to decipher, given the shared culture and other experiences. Proverbs provide a window through which the worldview of a people can be perceived, and the play *Emotan* presents instances of the use of aids in the creation and communication of compact messages among people who share a CG. Thus, when Esogban, in Act 1 Scene comments that:

> The content of a parcel is not known until it is opened (p. 8)

He is not referring to a physical parcel but is engaging the shared knowledge of proverbs held with the other members of the Oba's council. In King Orobiru's response to Chief Iyase (Act 1, Scene 1), he engages another proverb:

> When a man with diarrhoea, out of great pressure squats to defecate in your yard, you do not, out of sympathy allow him to finish (p. 9).

Orobiru is, by this statement, establishing a justification for his intended action to banish his brother Ogun from the Kingdom. The contextual situation of the proverb based on the CG shared with the chiefs made the proverbs perfectly understood by the listeners. There is nobody in doubt of the intentions of the King as none of them seeks clarifications. In other climes, such expressions as uttered by Orobiru could be taken literally, but the CG shared by the participants in the discourse makes the communication smooth. The nature of proverbs as an indication of CG is further exemplified in Act 2, Scene 2 when Ogun, and Irughe stand before their brother, King Orobiru. The brothers, at some point in their conversation resort to proverbs to communicate in the heat of the conversation. As Orobiru lashes out that "the fly never agrees that the sore is guilty" (p. 12), Irughe takes a cue from this proverb and decides to leave with Ogun, who has just been banished from the kingdom. Ogun, a dutiful brother and subject, but a strong warrior nonetheless retorts "He who throws the gauntlet must be prepared for war" (p. 12). Again, the contextual situation of these proverbs guarantees their unambiguous communicative value, both in the context in the play and of the play as the play continues, without a need for any further explanation on import or meanings these proverbial exchanges.

Lau, Tokofsky & Winick (2004) present proverbs as short, traditional utterances that encapsulate cultural truths and sum up recurrent social situations. This definition is brought to bear in *Emotan* as the use of proverbs in certain instances is an expression of cultural or philosophical truths which reflect social realities. For example, in Act 3 Scene 4, at the market place, while the women converse and pledge their support for Emotan and her resolution to ensure that justice is restored in Benin Kingdom, Adesuwa expresses that when Uwaifiokun fell out of favour with the King makers, who had perpetrated the injustice by crowning him King instead of his brother Ogun, the rightful heir, they would deal with him. He is therefore not out of arms way, as his situation could be likened to one where "the rain beats the pavement and the mud bench rejoices, forgetting it will soon be its turn" (p. 50). This proverb engages the co-participants' knowledge of the current happening in their society with which they can readily relate. The level of proverbs as an index of CG is again illustrated in Eki and Omosefe's exchanges:

> **Eki**: It doesn't matter *Iye*. We are not afraid. We are not doing anything illegal. You don't advice a child not to have protruding set of teeth, so long as he can get thick lips to cover them.
>
> **Omosefe:** Who cares? The kingmakers have called the masquerade – the masquerade is here dancing. Let them come out and watch it display…
>
> **Women:** They all laugh (pp. 51-52).

Eki ends the speech with a proverb while Omosefe responds with another proverb which elicited a common response (laughter) from the other women, signalling understanding and successive communication of idea.

Proverbs as used in *Emotan* are drawn from shared experiences which are cultural, environmental, and even political realities of the people. This echoes the perception of Adedimeji (2009: 545) on African proverbs as "… embracing the philosophical and socio-cultural values of Africans as they are derived from the culmination of African Cultural and social environment".

Stereotypes and Ideological Praxis

Croteau & Hoynes (2003: 160) posit that "ideology does not refer only to the beliefs held about the world, but also to the basic ways in which the world is defined". Consequently, ideology can be said to be a guide to individuals' and society's perception of issues as it is "a set of conscious and unconscious ideas that constitute one's goals, expectations and action". In a related submission, Fairclough (2003: 9) presents ideologies as "representations of aspects of the world which can be shown to contribute to establishing, maintaining and changing social relations of power, domination and exploitation"; they are thus implicit assumptions held in interaction. The above situates stereotypes as a part of the ideological make up of any group of society, seeing that it is their way of perceiving a person, group of people or particular ideas. In *Emotan*, stereotypes of women form a part of the CG as there are several references to the men "acting like a woman", which is consequent upon the stereotypical view about women. In Act 1 scene 3, at a meeting of Oba Uwaifiokun with the kingmakers, an argument ensues and as the Oba tries to wade into the altercation, he rebukes Chief Iyasere and Ihama:

> Enough, Enough my chiefs. This is very disgraceful. **Why do you quarrel and fight like women?...** (p. 14; *my emphasis*)

And in another response to the situation, he lashes out the chiefs:

> Enough. Stop I say. Enough of all this your quarrelling. **Are you women? ....** (p.15; *my emphasis*)

In the last part of the first excerpt, the king's words 'why do you quarrel and fight like women' suggests a stereotypical perception of women as being quarrelsome, petty and unable to settle their issues amicably. The men, on the other hand are always viewed as being in charge and in control of situations and it is therefore an aberration for them to bicker openly over issues. This is emphasised in the second excerpt.

The Esama, Iyasere and Oliha further stress this position in the same scene when they comment:

> **Esama**: I wonder why women can do nothing but quarrel, fight, gossip, backbite and slander. If your husband loves your mate better than you, why don't you look for a way to win his heart? I sometimes wonder why God had to waste his time creating women.
>
> **Iyasere**: So do I. They are called the weaker sex, yet they do dangerous things that beat our imagination. Can you imagine a woman, a mere woman plotting to take the life of an Oba?....
>
> **Oliha**: ...Women, women, they can overthrow nations, dethrone kings, bankrupt kingdoms, lead men to their downfall. They are evil. Worse than the devil himself (p. 17).

In this exchange, the chiefs launch an attack at the image of a woman, as they stereotypically choose Ubi, a bitter, jealous and wicked wife of an Oba in history who plotted to kill her husband, the Oba. The repercussion was that she was burnt to death with torches of firewood. In the same historical account however, another woman Ewere is presented as being calm, gentle and peaceful. But the chiefs' idea of a woman is Ubi, who is presented as an embodiment of wickedness. Their utterances in the above exchange depict not only their antipathy for any goodness in the women folk, but also their deep-seated perception of the female as a whole. Women are thus presented as nonentities occupying the men-space; conniving, pretentious creatures who are worse than the devil himself.

Other instances of the stereotypical lenses through which women are viewed in *Emotan* include that a woman cannot be self-sufficient and is expected to be supported by a man. Ihama's utterance in Act 1 scene 3, where the Oba is advised to *ba e igban[1]* Emotan and put her in his harem reflects this. He tells the Oba:

> **Ihama**: Your Majesty, I see no reason why Emotan, sluggish Emotan, a widow without the support of a man should be a source of concern to you (p. 22).

A woman is thus deemed incapable of self-sustainability and must be under the care of a man. This stereotypical perception is however refuted by the women in their conversation in the market:

> **Eki**: Iye, it is not that easy to cope.
> **Emotan**: It is very easy my sister Eki. By the time you come home with extra money made from your trading at the market, there will be extra funds to meet your children's needs without having to bother your husband for money all the time.
> **Adesuwa**: That is true. Then, there will be no more quarrelling in the home.
> **Imose**: No more "come and sell my clothes now," or "am I the Oba of Benin?"
> **Emotan**: Exactly. You will live in peace and harmony with your husband.
> **Eki**: That's true, that's true. So all this "where do you expect me to get money from?" will cease (pp. 25-26).

---

[1] To forcefully acquire.

The above excerpt shows that though the men regard themselves as being the provider in the home, they only give lip service to functioning in these roles in reality. They constantly complain of the women being too demanding.

The perception of men being below the men is further exemplified by King Uwaifiokun when he declares that he would rather abdicate the throne than dialogue with a woman.

> **Uwa**: What? Ohen my father, I, Oba Uwaifiokun, reason with a woman? No, never. No. I would rather give up the throne Isoken. Give up the throne and leave Benin (p. 36).

This stereotypical standpoint is not limited to the men. Having been a part of the same society and having shared in the cultural belief of what a woman's place is, even the women have come to accept themselves as weak and incapable of contributing anything consequential to a cause. Iriowen, one of the market women thus cautions Emotan as she advices her:

> **Iriowen**: Don't you think your actions may cause you so much problems you may not be able to handle? Emotan my dear, let's allow sleeping dogs lie. If Osa No ghodua wants any other prince to be the Oba of Benin, he will assist him and make a way for him.... He doesn't need you, a woman, to endanger your life to do it. Emotan, come to think of it, what assistance can you, a woman render that can help Okoro Ogun's son rule over Benin? (p. 46)

The above again typifies the overt classification of women as weak and ultimately subject to the men as perceived through the eyes of traditionally inclined women in the Benin society and by extension, the adherents of such traditions in our society today.

A further instantiation of the stereotypical perception of women in *Emotan* is the shared CG that women are sex objects, or at best, mates to warm the beds of their spouses. Here, the woman is presented as though she alone has the desire for sexual intimacy and this is considered as the fulfilment of her obligations as a wife. Oba Uwaifiokun in his conversation with Odoligie comments:

> **Uwaifiokun**: Odoligie, go to your bed and let me be alone. The bosom of your wife is itching for your warm embrace.... (p. 31)

And in another scene, Uwaifiokun, in anger, again denigrates women. He voices the traditional place of women as he puts his wife in her place with the reminder:

> **Uwaifiokun**: ... How can a woman pry into a man's affairs? Did you mother ever ask your father such questions? Who gave you the right to question me Isoken, who? Your duty in the palace is to warm my bed, bear my children, rear them and that is all. You hear, Isoken, that is all (p. 34)

The above exchange foregrounds the shared situational and cultural knowledge of the traditional role and place of the woman. It is based on this assumed shared cultural and experiential knowledge that Oba Uwaifiokun asks his wife Isoken if her mother had ever asked her father such questions: it is shared knowledge that women, considering their place, have no right to question their husbands over certain issues. The same excerpt also encapsulates the women in the light of her perceived

84

worth: warm the man's bed, have children and take care of the child.

This limiting standpoint of a woman's worth is perhaps a spin-off of the patriarchal make up of Nigeria and Africa, and in a refutal, A. Philips posits that a woman is a woman in herself and should not be judged by her relationships. In his words "... the woman's essential worth stems from her common humanity and does not depend on other relationships of her life" (1987: 68). The stereotypical approach to the treatment and perception is thus queried and challenged.

Belief in the Metaphysical as an Index of Common Ground

A shared phenomenon which co-constitutes the CG of Africans is the belief in the metaphysical and the ancestral. Africans are considered traditional, not only in the cultural orientations such as it relates to food, community and other ideological considerations, but also as it concerns their ingrained believe in the existence of the metaphysical and the ability of the metaphysical, and by extension, the ancestral to decide events and happenings in the human realm. Such shared cultural knowledge is hinged on the importance that Africans place on religion. There is therefore seen to be a direct correlation between the religion and the belief in the ancestral / metaphysical, as the metaphysical beings are often times regarded as gods or spirits that have the power to make things work for humans or punish them for their misdeeds. This belief tends to guide the attitude and dealings of human beings who live with this consciousness.

In *Emotan*, references are made to ancestors, ancestral gods, gods of Benin, spirit of good luck and the 'gods of my father'. These ancestors are believed to protect the people from their enemies and any impending evil. In Act 1, scene 3 for instance, Esogban, one of the kingmakers assures King Uwaifiokun and his fellow kingmakers of the protection of the gods. He says "...have no fears, our ancestors will protect us against the forces of our enemies" (p. 15). These gods of the land and the ancestors are also deemed to be capable of granting the wishes of the people and giving them prosperity. The market women thus pray to these gods for bountiful sales.

> **Iriowen**: May the gods of our land send us buyers today o. May they give us a bright and perfect day to carry out our business
> **Market Women**: Ise e oo (p. 39).

As an indication of the communal believe that is in force in the above excerpt, the market women all chorus "*ise e o*" (trans: so may it be) to the prayer offered by Iriowen, signifying their agreement to the prayer and also an understanding of the prayer and its essence. Iriowen's prayer can be seen to be invoking the spirit of good luck for their business for the day, the same spirit that Emotan refers to her interaction with the market women later in the text (p. 80). She reminds them that the spirit is capable of being grieved and can disappear. The people of Benin therefore share the CG of the existence of these spirits and gods and their abilities: they can help (p. 49, 64), protect (p. 84), guide (p. 68), and also bear witness (p. 9). There is however the other side of these spirits: they can unleash judgement as their wrath can be incurred. This knowledge is thus seen to guide the people into acting right as exemplified by Irughe's utterance (p. 12) and Imose's speech (p. 41). The wrath of the ancestors was not to be trifled with.

Use of Contrast for the Proposal of Alternative Ideologies

Common Ground is indexed through the use of contrast for the proposal of alternative ideologies, and for querying the existing order of male superiority as well as highlighting the shortcomings of the patriarchal system in force. Contrast as used in *Emotan* involves the comparison of different things; and juxtaposition with the intent of highlighting the difference between the things or ideas being compared. The women described by the kingmakers as contentious, deceitful and evil are the same women who bring the Ewere leaves, the leaves of peace, the leaves of favour. On arrival, Iriowen announces on behalf of the women, "Your Majesty, Here is peace, favour and blessings we have brought from our ancestors to you..." (p. 18) and thereafter offers prayers for the peace and prosperity of Benin Kingdom.

Ihama's conversation with Oba Uwa refers to Emotan as a "sluggish woman, a widow without the support of any man" (p. 22) who should not be a source of concern to the king. Yet, out of fear of her popularity and the realisation of the power she wields among the women, Ihama advises the King to forcefully, in the traditional way (*ba e igban*), put Emotan in his harem, so as to ensure control over her. The foregrounded use of contrast here however reveals that if indeed Emotan is as helpless as they make her to be, it is not necessary to gain control over here and prevent her from trying to help Ogun reclaim his throne. Again, at the meeting convened in Chief Iyasere's house, the chiefs warn the men and women of the danger that Emotan poses, after having earlier instructed the men to convince their wives against supporting her (pp. 56-57). This further shows that the men believe in the intellectual ability of Emotan and as a symbol of women's authority. This echoes Ryan's (1988: 24) submission that "women are full human beings capable of participation and leadership in the full range of human activities: intellectual,

87

social, sexual, spiritual and economic". The savvy of the African woman in leading others and organizing events, both in home affairs and in the affairs of the state are thus highlighted here.

In page 59 of *Emotan*, the exchanges among Imade, Iriowen and Adesuwa question the existing order of male superiority which absolves the men even when they do wrong but subjects the women to punishments. Imade's speech resists this position and asks "are the ancestral spirits discriminatory? Are they meant to protect only the interest of our men?" (p. 59). Imade reminds the women of their ideal state of affairs: Both the men and women swore to the ancestral spirits, when they got married, to be faithful to each other. The fulfilment of this should therefore not be one sided and any defaulter, be it a man or a woman, must be made to face the same penalties. This knowledge, though expected to be in the core common ground of the interlocutors, is treated as emergent common ground in this instance as Imade introduces it as some form of information to be accommodated in the course of the conversation. Consequently, Imade suggests an alternative ideology; one in which men are women are culpable when they err, and one in which there are no scapegoats or sacred cows. An ideology of fairness and equality as against one of suppression and oppression is thus proposed.

Conclusion

By and large, we have shown that the communicative intentions in *Emotan* are entrenched in the context in which the play is set and the contexts created and enacted in the play. These contexts are the sources of Common Ground which is the totality of shared experiences and beliefs held by interlocutors prior to the interaction which are brought into the conversations. Given the dynamic nature of Common Ground, information that might not be shared prior to the conversation are supplied, updated and consequently accommodated as shared in the course of the conversation.

Common Ground in *Emotan* has consequently been established as being fuelled by cultural knowledge and beliefs, shared experiences and situational provisions and limitations in conversations. This is realised and played out in the play text using proverbs which are at the core of the common ground shared by the people. The proverbs easily communicate deep meanings among interactors in *Emotan*. The shared understanding of stereotypes and belief in the metaphysical are also the basis for the establishment and reflection of CG as they provide some form of platform for the understanding of certain utterances and attitudes in the interactions in the play text. These features are very essential for the build up and amplification of the overall meaning embedded in the play text as they also serve as a lens through which the cultural, social and societal beliefs and expectations that interlocutors bring into interactions can be perceived and understood. Ultimately, the study has accounted for the workings of Common Ground in *Emotan* and how it is instantiated, updated and explored in the play text.

REFERENCES

Adedimeji, M. (2009). "A universal pragmatic analysis of Nigerian proverbs in Ola Rotimi's Kurunmi", in A. Odebunmi et al (ed.), *Language, gender and politics: A festschrift for Yissa Kehinde Yusuf. Lagos*: Concept Publications, pp.545-547.

Adeoti, O. (2015). *Common ground and ideology in editorial cartoons in three Nigerian newspapers*. Unpublished doctoral thesis, Department of English, University of Ilorin.

Adeoti, O. (2016). "Proverbs and national development: A pragma-lexico-semantic analysis of selected proverbs about children", in S. T. Babatunde, U. E. Josiah & M. Ekah (eds.), *English Language and Literature in Non-Native Environments: Issues, Patterns and Preferences. A Festschrift in Honour of Professor David Jowitt.* University of Uyo: Department of English, pp. 263-275.

Babatunde, S. T. (2007). "A speech acts analysis of Christian religious speeches", in A. Odebunmi & A. O. Babajide, (eds.), *Style in religious communication in Nigeria.* Muenchen: Lincoln Europa, pp. 48-89.

Bach, K and Harnish, R. (1979). *Linguistic communication and speech acts.* Cambridge: Mass. MIT Press.

Clark, H. H. (1996). *Using language.* Cambridge: Cambridge University Press.

Clark, H. H. (2006). "Context and Common Ground", in Keith Brown (ed.), *Encyclopedia of language and linguistics* (2nd ed., Vol. 3). Oxford: Elsevier, pp. 105-108.

Clark, H. H. (2009). "Context and common ground", in J. L. Mey, (ed.), *Concise Encyclopedia of Pragmatics.* Oxford: Elsevier, pp. 116-119.

Croteau, D & Hoynes, W. (2003). *Media / Society: Industries, images and audiences* (3rd ed.). USA: Pine Forge Press.

Enfield, N. (2008). "Common ground as a resource for social affiliation", in I. Kecskes & J. Mey, (eds.), *Intention, common ground and the egocentric speaker-hearer.* Berlin: Mouton de Gruyter, pp. 183-224.

Evwierhoma, M. I. E. (2009). "Rising Profile of a Female Dramatist Irene Isoken Salami and New Nigerian Woman-Centred Drama", in https://www.ajol.info/index.php/cajtms/article/download/76616/ 67063, pp. 41-51 (retrieved 10 August 2018).

Fairclough, N. (2001). *Language and power*. London: Pearson Education Ltd.

Fetzer, A. (2011) "Pragmatics as a linguistic concept", in W. Bublitz & N. R. Norrick, (eds.), *Foundations of Pragmatics* (pp. 23-50). Berlin: De Grutyer Mouton.

Horton, W. (2008). *A memory based approach to common ground and audience design*, in I. Kecskes & J. Mey (eds.), *Intention, common ground and the egocentric speaker-hearer*. Berlin: Mouton de Gruyter, pp. 189-223.

Kecskes, I. (2014). *Intercultural pragmatics*. Oxford: Oxford University Press.

Lau, K., Tokofsky, P. & Winick S. (2004). *What goes around comes around: The circulation of proverbs in contemporary life*. Logan, Utah: Utah State University.

Lewis, D. (1979). "Scorekeeping in a language game". *Journal of Philosophical Logic*. 8, pp. 339-359.

Philips, A. (1987). *Feminism and Equality: Readings in social and political thought*. Oxford: Basil Blackwell Ltd.

Ryan, R. & Van Zyl S. (1988). *An introduction to contemporary feminist theory*. Johannesburg: Ad Donker Ltd.

Salami, I. I. (2001). *Emotan*: A Benin Heroine. Nigeria: Mazlink Nigeria Limited.

Wheelwright, P. (1975). *Metaphor and reality*. Bloomington and London: Indiana University Press.

GENDER ISSUES IN STELLA OYEDEPO'S *BRAIN HAS NO GENDER*

Florence. A. ELEGBA

Introduction

Gender and cultural studies have been serious subjects of literary debate and criticism for some decades. Several female African / Nigerian writers have emerged to contribute to the debate by projecting a positive image of African woman as indispensable partner on the road to the development of the continent in general and to national development of Nigeria in particular. Among the Nigerian female playwrights are Zulu Sofola, Tess Onwueme, Catherine Acholonu, Irene Salami-Agunloye, Osita Ezenwanebe, Stella Oyedepo, Julie Okoh, Folashade Ogunrinde, Chinyere Okafor, Onyeka Onyekuba, and Tracie Utoh-Ezeajugh.

The works of these female playwrights are reactions to the negative portrayal of female characters by most male playwrights in Nigeria. They decry the portrayal of females as sex objects, dancers to entertain men, witches, and many other retrogressive cultural emblems that keep the female gender at the lowest ebb of the ladder of development in the society. They write against all forms of discrimination against women, violence against women, and women deprivation in socio, economic, political and religious matters. Their works are out for feminine social, economic, political, religious and cultural transformation which will dignify the female gender identity and reposition women positively in a male dominated society.

Highlighting the intention of African Women writers in the rebranding discourse, Zainab Alkali (2012: 16) asserts that:

The women writers, therefore, have to recreate African women's image by creating characters that preferably in male dominated professions; the sciences and the social sciences, women who are not only economically independent, but psychologically strong and as ambitious as the men.

Several ideological schools on gender studies exist to address female gender related issues. Predominant among them is Feminism. Many scholars have defined feminism, including Barrow and Milburn (1990:.128) who sees it as "a label for commitment or movement to achieve equality for women". Feminism seeks equal opportunities for women in society. Cuddon (1991: 338) sees feminism from literary point of view, as "an attempt to describe and interpret (or reinterpret) women's experiences as depicted in various kinds of literature", while Ogundipe-Leslie (2007: 547) defines feminism as "an ideology of women; anybody of social philosophy about women". Sotunsa (2008: 14) also asserts that whether as a theory or a social or political movement, "feminism focuses on women's experiences and highlights various forms of oppression which the female gender is subjected to in the society".

In a similar vein, Umoren (2002) quoted in Arinde (2010: 458) opines that "feminism decries in very strong terms the subjugation of women by men and demands for the authenticity of the liberation of women from male domination both in the institution of marriage and the larger society". Seen as an ideology with emphasis on the rights and position of women in society, Lawal (2015: 131) describes feminism as "an ideology in which significant attention is paid to women's rights as well as their position in society. It advocates equality between men and women especially regarding political, social, and economic considerations".

A careful examination of all definitions and descriptions of feminism reveals that it is a theory or an ideology that strives to achieve the emancipation of the female gender from all forms of retrogressive socio-economic and cultural practices which exclude women from functioning effectively in a male dominated society. It also seeks equal acceptability and opportunity with the male gender.

Principles of Feminism

Lawal (2015: 133-134) cites Sheila (1980) to highlight some beliefs, values, attitude, aims and aspirations of feminism as a theory and a socio-political movement:

- Feminists value women in and of themselves, not in the hypocritical fashion of male-dominated environment;
- Feminists value and prize the fact of being women as much as being human. They see themselves as strong, capable, intelligent and successful ethical human beings;
- Feminists value autonomy for themselves as individuals and for women as a group who are developing their own political, social, and economic destinies;
- Feminists reject separation of human qualities into categories-one for men and one for women-and the value of one of those categories better than the other. For instance, male characteristics of aggression, power and competition are celebrated, while the

female characteristics of compassion, tenderness and compromise are viewed as weak and ridiculed;

- Feminists believe that attitude regarding women in many cultures are false and often based on myth, ignorance, and fear and therefore should be replaced with reality and knowledge created by women first for women and for all people;
- Feminists point out denial of their rights as human for centuries, rights such as voting, earnings and freedom to determine to bear children or not etc; and
- Finally, feminists recognize women's strength in the face of oppression and are optimistic about the possibilities of change.

From the above, it can be accepted that a feminist does not subscribe to the ideology of fatalism or determinism of social order; rather she strives to remove all obstacles debarring her from maximizing her potentials in a male dominated society.

Forms of Feminism

Feminism has myriads of variants ranging from Western feminism, Africana feminism, Cultural feminism, Marxist/ Socialist feminism, Radical feminism, Liberal feminism, Humanist feminism, Analytical feminism, Lesbian feminism to Nego-feminism promoted by Obiora Nnaemeka. However, because of the inadequacy of feminism in solving the different problems faced by African woman, Hudson-Weems (1998: 24) advances the idea that race and class-based oppression is of greater import than gender-based oppression, especially when feminism addresses issues that are directly related and beneficial to white women. Hence, there are other related concepts on female gender studies. Among such concepts is Womanism coined by Alice Walker in 1984. These forms of feminism are briefly introduced.

One of the more popular concepts of feminism is womanism, which is a theory that explains the day to day experiences of women in society, especially in relation to the numerous problems women encounter in a male dominated society and how to solve them. African-American writer Alice Walker defines a womanist as "a woman who loves another woman, sexually and / or non-sexually". The womanist appreciates and prefers women's culture, women's emotional flexibility (values tears as a natural counterbalance of laughter), and women strength... (1983: xii). Womanism is rooted in the racial and gender oppression of the African-American woman, leading to the position by Yacim et al (2015: 28) that it fails to "address the problems of African woman; rather it addresses issues that are more sociologically grounded in Western culture, e.g. lesbianism..." Because Walker's womanism is inadequate in capturing the African women experiences satisfactorily, other variants of womanist theories emerged. One of such is Black Feminism or Africana Womanism developed by African-American scholar, Clenora Hudson-Weems.

Other forms include African Womanism, which "is grounded in African culture, and therefore, it necessarily focuses on the unique experiences, struggles, needs, and desires of Africana women" (Hudson-Weems, 1993, 24) Apart from Africana womanism, other African-oriented feminine ideologies are Molara Ogundipe-Leslie's African-centred STIWANISM (Social Transformation in Africa Including Women), Obioma Nnaemeka's Nego-feminism and Catherine Acholonu's Motherism. These are ideologies that are traditionally African as observed by Evwierhoma (2015: 257), because "they promote

96

the Africanness of women as members of local or global community, and agents of nurture, whether through change, role performance or affirmation of self and race". Evwierhoma argues that Nnaemeka considers negotiation as a means of working towards common and not individual goals in order to promote collaboration between male and female genders. She sees Nego-feminism as a response to Euro-American idea of feminism which is gender-separatist rather than complementary. Evwierhoma (2015: 257) however regards Stiwanism as a theory that is "against the common exclusion of African women from global discourses of change and transformation". Stiwanism therefore signifies the importance of inclusiveness and participation of women in discourses, programmes, and activities geared towards social change and transformation. Exclusion of women from matters that concern them and their children in the changing world will be an aberration.

Motherism is another important theory of feminism developed by Catherine Acholonu. Acholonu (1995: 110-111) defines Motherism as "a multidimensional theory which involves the dynamics of ordering, recording, creating structures, building and rebuilding in cooperation with mother nature at all levels of human endeavour". Motherist theory advocates that a woman should rediscover and re-actualise herself, but not to the disadvantage of her home and family. Acholonu declares that Motherism is about love, tolerance, service, and mutual cooperation of both male and female sexes without the aggression and violent confrontation that was associated with radical feminism. Motherism, similar to Stiwanism, emphasises the complementary role of the African woman in society building. The essence of Motherism is "partnership, cooperation, tolerance, love, understanding and patience" (Acholonu, 1995:.112). Motherism therefore captures the essence of the

97

African woman as she relates with her God, the environment, and the male gender. A Motherist appreciates the diversity of human nature and respects the views and weakness of others. Ezenwanebe (2008: 185) commenting on these ideologies asserts that they:

> are united in the quest for complementarity of the sexes based on the co-existence of men and women in equal dignity, opportunities, and privileges unlike the Western feminism which works for equality of sexes achieved through a battle of the sexes aimed at upturning the structure in gender relations to the benefit of women.

In a similar vein, Uchendu (2016: 29-42) describes Ogundipe-Leslie's Stiwanism, Acholonu's Motherism, Mary Kolawole's Womanism (devised from Walker's Womanism), Nnaemeka's Negofeminism and Adimora-Ezeigbo's Snail Sense Feminism as strands of African feminism with a common ground of situating women struggle within African cultural context and upholding "the principle of accommodation of African males". According to him, African feminism seeks to challenge all the socio-cultural and religious barriers which patriarchal African societies have imposed on women leading to their age long subjugation. African feminism relates the psychology of being a woman in African environment. In essence, African feminism desires an African society where developmental potentials of women will be maximized without any socio-cultural and religious barriers. As part of the efforts of female playwrights to recreate and reposition the African female gender's image in a male dominated society along the understanding of the above concepts, this chapter explores Stella Oyedepo's effort at recreating and repositioning the girl-child on the same pedestal as her male counterpart in her play *Brain Has No Gender*.

A Feminist Reading of *Brain Has No Gender*

In *Brain Has No Gender*, Stella Oyedepo explores the themes of girl-child education, forced child-marriage, retrogressive societal customs / norms, beliefs and traditions. She emphasises the importance of girl-child education as the bedrock of bridging the gap created between the male and female genders in the African society. She advocates through the drama that prejudicial beliefs and negative cultural practices that tend to keep women relegated can be removed through education. This thesis of the importance of education is propounded at the beginning of the play:

> **3rd Voice:** (Rises up) …Let us force open the door of knowledge. Education shall liberate us from suppression. Education shall lift the veil of ignorance from the eyes of all women. Women must go through life with greater visibility!
>
> **4th Voice:** Yes, we agree. Education shall rescue us. We too shall join the men in exploring the depths of knowledge. We shall not accept to be mere fetchers of water and hewers of wood. We can do more than housekeepers or glorified slaves.
>
> **5th Voice:** (Rises up) But the question is, can we do it? Can a woman's brain cope with scientific knowledge and investigations, for example?
>
> **6th Voice:** Women, yes, we have the grey matter to cope. The human brain does not have gender differentiation. Nature is impartial in this regard. A woman's brain does not function less than a man's. No gender difference in the human brain, I repeat. The female has equal power as the male.

7th Voice: (Rises up) Women, let us rise to the challenge. We can do it! And we shall do it (pp. 3-5).

Stella Oyedepo demonstrates the liberating potential of Western education as she enacts the story of Osomo whose father Alani forcefully withdraws from school to marry his octogenarian friend, Kelani. He could not see the importance of educating a girl-child and concludes that education creates pride and insubordination in a girl.

> What is the use of a woman's education? Is she not going to waste it in the kitchen? Once you educate a woman, she can no longer be a good wife. She only becomes a swollen-headed. I have seen examples even in this village. Look at teacher's wife, she is very arrogant just because she 'knows small book'. She walks like this, (*demonstrates*) puffing like *tolotolo*[1] (p.31).

The injustice against the girl-child indicates the lack of voice of the African women in matters that directly affect them. They are left in the dark on issues that could adversely affect their future. Further, women are blamed and held responsible for having female children instead of having male children, as tangentially referenced in Alani's decision to stop Osomo's education and to send her mother back to her parent's home for giving birth to a girl. Alani's decision is therefore borne out of his frustration after having sixteen female children from seven wives. In desperation for a male child, he is prepared to do anything; for instance, he offers yam and hen to Ifalami (the Ifa Priest) as sacrifices to have male child. The Ifa priest instructs him to

---

[1] Turkey

dance around the town in his best garment so Orunmila can grant his wishes. He sees dancing around the town as a simple assignment to shake off the curse of having only female children compared with the previous prescription of feasting on faeces of a pig and keeping a toad in his pants, which were the earlier prescriptions. He confesses this in his dialogue with the Ifa priest who believes that his inability to have a male child is the handiwork of witches and wizards (p.10). Alani eagerly narrates his gruesome experience while searching for a male child:

> I tell you Baba, mine has been an unusual ill-luck… Baba, is it not a bitter irony that I, the same one whose masculine power is stronger than that of a horse, should father sixteen female children with no male child, not a premature one as an evidence of my potency?… And what have I not done to remove the curse? Me, Alani. I have done un-imaginable things. There was a time I had to feast on the faeces of a pig for seven days. Can you imagine that! At another time, I had to endure the creepy sensation of a toad in my pants for three days… so that my sperm might change into male forming ones. Nothing came out of this gruesome experience. Despite all my efforts, my seven wives keep delivering female children (p.10).

Alani dances around the town distributing akara balls as sacrifices to appease witches and wizards so that he could have male children. He attributes the interest of the witches in cursing him with female children to his success as a farmer. Oyedepo exposes the self-imposed heart-ache of some African men in their desperate bid to have a male child irrespective of the scientific reasons or implications such as sterility or other

101

biological reasons. These are some of the retrogressive cultural beliefs and practices that hamper national development.

In Movement Two, Oyedepo presents Awele and her daughter Osomo in the maternity ward of the hospital for the first time because there are indications that the baby could be a boy. Previously, Awele had not been allowed to give birth at the hospital where she would receive a proper care, but this birth is different; there is a prediction of a set of male triplets. Oyedepo highlights here the general uncaring attitude of men towards the birth of female children. The interactions between Awele, Osomo and Alani, and the nurse in this movement is a revelation of the lack of professionalism as well as lack of empathy among Nigerian professionals who are also female, which is remarkable especially as the nurse, in this case, is a woman who is in the same social and political position as Awele. To the pregnant woman who has had a protracted labour for five days, she reacts:

> (*Rather callously*) Heh... Stop it... Look at her barking like a dog. (*Awele yells the more*) I say shut up! Stop this loud yelling! Don't you know you are disturbing people's peace, mooing like that? Like a cow? Where is your card?... Didn't she attend ante-natal? Bush woman! You still don't realize the importance of ante natal care? (p. 16).

Even though there is a message in women's attendance of ante-natal clinic and the need to maintain absolute silence in maternity/ hospital premises, suggested in the script, the nurse's reaction apart from being unethical reveals the effect of poor education on women. Awele is illiterate and cannot read the signs, the nurse is ignorant of her duty of care. Oyedepo uses this scene to expose the attitudes of some nurses to patients and their attendants or helpers in the hospitals with the intention of

102

correcting such anti-feminine attitude among the nursing professionals.

Nonetheless, Alani drums and dances around the maternity ward in expectation of the arrival of his set of male triplets as Ifalami has predicted. The triplets are female, and in his disappointment, he banishes Awele to her father's house. Ironically, though Awele suffers for giving birth to female children, the reason actually lies in Alani's inability to produce the determining male chromosomes needed to create male children. Oyedepo exposes the African man's attitude towards childbirth, which is rooted in this ignorance. Scientifically, the sex of a child is determined by the fusion of XY chromosomes from the male with the XX chromosomes from the female. If the man's X chromosome fuses with the woman's X chromosome, a female child results; however, if it is the Y chromosome from the man that fuses with X chromosome from the woman, the result is a male child. Alani blames his seven wives for giving birth to female children without acknowledging the male causative factor.

Alani forces Osomo his daughter to marry Octogenerian Kelani in a seemingly unrealistic match; Kelani is in his eighties; a man old enough to be Osomo's grandfather. This is a commentary on the reality of what happens in the society however. There are numerous newspaper reports and court cases of men in their seventies defiling girls of as young as eight or ten years old. There are equally reports of child marriage in Nigeria whish Oyedepo uses this play to satirise. Osomo sobs throughout the period of the ceremony, a sign her father interprets to mean cultural acceptance of the marriage, as brides usually keen and weep on the way to their husband's house as a traditional form of saying goodbye to their family. Still, she is determined to free herself from the marriage. Her actions are not dramatized but

Kelani reports to his friends Ejide, Olude and Kanmi that "Osomo has broken my testicles [...] maiming one's husband's organ and rendering it useless, is unheard of, unheard of on a wedding night..." (pp. 35-36). The injury caused to the testicles symbolises a breaking away from the retrogressive culture of forced child-marriage as this enables Osomo to escape from Kelani's house. She resurfaces eight years later as a medical doctor, after graduating as the best student in her university.

Education is important, and success is not dependent on whether the brain is male or female, but on other factors that are not gender based. Oyedepo uses a debate on the university canpus between two characters of the opposite sex to expose the neutrality of the brain. That is, the human brain is not gender biased and the news of Osomo's brilliant performance at the medical school.

> **Funmi:** I am saying it again, girls or women are not as weak as you men make yourselves to believe.
>
> **Jide:** Come on Funmi, I think you women are becoming rather swollen headed. Now think of scientific inventions and discoveries of monumental significance, was there any one made by a woman? Isaac Newton, Benjamin Franklin, John Thomson and most of the world's great scientists were men.
>
> **Funmi:** That may be true but the question is, can't women do it? Were these discoveries and inventions made with male organs? Pardon my vulgar language. Now are you trying to prove that the possession of a male organ is an index of a higher mental capability? I am saying emphatically that the brain has no gender... I am

> trying to prove to you that a woman's brain is in
> no way inferior to a man's. Of course, the brain
> has no gender (p. 41).

Oyedepo argues further through Funmi that "if women have
equal opportunities as men, then, they will perform and
contribute as much as men..." (p. 44). The appearance of Sanmi
and Lanre to announce the excellent performance of Osomo who
has won sixteen prizes with the best result ever in the entire
country boosts Funmi's position on women's ability to attain
excellence. She admires Osomo's brilliant performance which
brings glory and honour to the womenfolk. Osomo attributes her
success to her determination to succeed after escaping from
home:

> You all know my story. If I hadn't escaped from
> home, I would have led a wasted life as a grand
> papa's wife. I would have gone into debris of times
> without realizing what I would have become. You
> know my father wanted to force me into early
> marriage (p. 48).

Osomo's appearance back in the village as a medical doctor
thrills the teacher, her benefactor who had encouraged her whilst
in school. It also humbles and excites her father who in disbelief
declares:

> Osomo, a child in a million. A daughter who has
> done what a thousand sons cannot do. I hope you
> have forgiven me. When you ran away, I thought you
> had ran with a man. Osomo, God has been with you.
> What a male child cannot do, you have done... I am
> going to feast in this house for twenty-one days to
> compensate for my years of mourning. I have
> mourned and mourned that God didn't give me a

male child. Is Osomo not greater than one hundred men? A doctor... a doctor. Now I am a most happy man. I thank my creator. I thank Tisha, I thank Tisha (p. 53).

Alani seeks forgiveness and promises to withdraw all her daughters from their husbands' houses to go back to school. He also begs Awele his first wife and Osomo's mother to return to her matrimonial home and take her rightful place. He decides to tender an apology to his in-laws for his ignorance. The villagers see Osomo's arrival as Godsent to attend to their ailments in the community and in particular her father's hernia.

The play ends on a happy note as the seven Voices display various scientific gadgets singing and charging women to rise and improve their lot. They chant furiously many times the slogan 'Brain Has No Gender'. Oyedepo, using this play, successfully contributes to gender discourse in African literature by upholding the virtues of determination, resilience, hard work and breaking away from all retrogressive societal norms and traditions which keep the African woman perpetually down in poverty, penury, and slavery to her male counterpart. This is one of the main manifestos of feminism.

Conclusion

This play encourages women in Africa and in Nigeria in particular to shake off cultural practices that hinder women from acquiring empowering education. Through the events, situation, characters, dialogue, songs, chants, music, and dance, Oyedepo successfully presents the significance of acquiring education as necessary to bridging the gap between male and female gender in Nigeria. As a feminist, Stella Oyedepo prescribes in this play that the female gender should radically break off every obstacle against attaining highest possibilities in life. She sees determination to acquire Western education and diligence as important recipes in climbing the ladder of success and to change one's fortune in life especially when nature has not favoured the male over and above the female gender, as far as the human brain is concern. The human brain has no gender.

Evwierhoma (2009: 245) asserts that Stella Oyedepo's *Brain Has No Gender* "is a play that is against the denial of the right of females to education, forced marriage, and the customs and practices that subjugate women". Commenting on Osomo's success in school which changes her position in her father's house, in her community and the larger society, Sarki (2015: 221) maintains that justice and equitable society is achievable through women's hard work and education when he says that, "the balkanized identity of women can be redefined and denied rights reclaimed through education, which is the bedrock of knowledge".

REFERENCES

Alkali, Z. (2012). "Gender politics and sexual dynamics, imaging men in African women's writing: The quest for identity and integrity", in Yerima, A. and Aliu, S. (eds.), *Gender politics, women writings and Film in Northern Nigeria*. Ibadan: Kraft Books, pp. 11-20.

Acholonu, C. (1995). *Motherism: The Afrocentric alternative to feminism*. Owerri: Afa Publications.

Arinde, T.S. (2010). "Repositioning women for the promotion of global peace: A case study of *The Wives Revolt* and *Queen Ghasengeh*", in Ododo, S. E. and Bodunde, C. (eds.), *Obafemi Confab Book of Proceedings on the International Conference on*

African Literature and Theatre. Abuja: National Commission for Museums and Monuments, pp. 457-475.

Barrow, R. and Geoffrey, M. (1990). *A critical dictionary of education concepts*, 2nd Edition. New York: Harvester Wheatsheaf.

Cuddon, D. (1991). *A dictionary of literary theory*, 3rd Edition. Oxford: Blackwell.

Echendu, N.F. (2016). *African feminism: A study of selected works of Akachi Adimora-Ezeigbo*. (An unpublished PhD. Thesis submitted to the Department of English, University of Ilorin).

Evwierhoma, M. I. (2009). "Theater, Minority Rights and the Gender Question: Whither Nigerian Female Dramatist", in Asagba, A.O. (ed.), *Theatre and minority rights: Perspectives on the Niger Delta*. Ibadan: Kraft Books, pp. 238-252.

Evwierhoma, M. (2015). "Interview by Methuselah Jeremiah", in Jeremiah, M. and Evwierhoma, M. (eds.), *Snapshots of the female ethos: essays on women in drama and culture in Africa*. Lagos: Concept Publications Limited, pp. 247-270.

Ezenwanebe, O. (2008). "Women, economic empowerment and Nigerian drama: Implication for economic and human development", *Femi Osofisan International Conference on Performance Proceedings*. Ibadan: University of Ibadan, pp. 184-193.

Hudson-Weems, C. (1998). *Africana womanism: reclaiming ourselves*. Troy, MI: Bedford Pub.

Kolawole, M. (1997). *Womanism and African consciousness*. Trenton: African World Press.

Lawal, H. O. (2015). Feminism in the drama of Zulu Sofola. In Jeremiah, M. and Evwierhoma, M. (Eds.)., *Snapshots of the female ethos: essays on women in drama and culture in Africa*. Lagos: Concept Publications Limited, pp. 131-145.

Ogundipe-Leslie, M. (1994). *Recreating ourselves: African women and critical transformation*. Trenton: African World Press.

Ogundipe-Leslie, M. (2007). Stiwanism: Feminism in an African Context. In Olaniyan, T. and Quayson, A. (Eds.)., *African literature: An anthology of criticism and theory*. Malden: Blackwell, pp. 542-550.

Oyedepo, S. (2001). *Brain Has No Gender*. Ilorin: Delstar Publishers.

Sarki, P.E. (2015). "The denial of girl-child education in Nigeria: Oyedepo's counter-attack in *Brain Has No Gender*", in Jeremiah, M. and Evwierhoma, M. (eds.), *Snapshots of the female ethos: essays on women in drama and culture in Africa*. Lagos: Concept Publications Limited, pp. 212-227.

Sheila, R. (1980). *Issues in feminism: A first course in women studies*. Boston: Houghton Mifflin.

Sotunsa, M. (2008). *Feminism and gender discourse: The African experience*. Sagamu: Asaba.

Yacim, R, Okposio, E. & Ogbeche, S. (2015). "Gender complementarity as exemplified in Sunnie Ododo's *To Return from the Void* and *Vanishing Vapour*", in Jeremiah, M. and Evwierhoma, M. (eds.), *Snapshots of the female ethos: essays on women in drama and culture in Africa*. Lagos: Concept Publications Limited, pp. 24-39.

FEMALE REPRESENTATION AND OBJECTIFICATION IN ZULU SOFOLA'S *THE SWEET TRAP*

Bassey Nsa EKPE

Introduction

"The early period of playwriting in Nigeria was dominated by Wole Soyinka, J.P. Clark, and Ola Rotimi. Zulu Sofola only emerged a little later" (Azunwo and Omovwiomo, 2015: 6). They raise the important fact that almost every play of these three forerunners celebrates the power and glory of highly drawn heroes, ranging from Kurunmi in *Kurunmi* and Odewale in *The Gods are not to Blame* by Ola Rotimi; Olunde in *Death and the King's Horseman* and Kongi in *Kongi's Harvest* by Wole Soyinka; and Ozidi in *Ozidi* by J.P. Clark. The female characters placed alongside these heroes are weak, choiceless, almost invisible and insignificant. Mosadinwin, the wife of Kurunmi is an example of this. In Soyinka's plays, there are Sadiku in *The Lion and the Jewel*, Rola in *A Dance of the Forests*, Iyaloja and Bride in *Death and the King's Horseman*, and Amope in *The Trials of Brother Jero*. These characters do not play any heroic roles but are mostly objectified as anti-heroes or foils to the main characters; or as temptresses or wives. The stylistic bent of these early writers privilege male heroes in contrast to the drama of later male playwrights, such as Femi Osofisan who does not follow the conventions of the early male playwrights in their traditional sociological portrayal of women. His work goes against replicating tradition; rather, he refines tradition and elevates the role of women in his plays by giving them positive and significant characterisation in plays such as *Once upon Four Robbers, Fires Burn and Die Hard,* and *Morountodun.*

110

Zulu Sofola joined the group of writers with *The Disturbed Peace of Christmas*, which was published in 1991. Though a female, Sofola's entry into the playwriting scene did not alter the image of women in literary drama. Her writing reaffirmed the supposed superiority and supremacy of men over women. Sofola's plays in addition gave domination to the image of men in the society. Her work highlights the regular conflict of old and new culture, with the old ideology always overcoming the new forms. Sofola writes from the perspective of a traditionalist; her plays overwhelm and enchant the sacredness of traditions, and her dramaturgy undermines any of her character that goes against tradition. From her portrayal, the inviolability of tradition must be maintained and respected at all cost even in the face of its inertness and retrogressive nature. In some of her plays, attempts by women to break free from established traditional sacredness incur a vicious critique. In *The Sweet Trap* for example, male supremacy over the female takes centre stage. This situation is understandable in form of Clara's character who attempts to challenge an age-old injunction that the husband's word is law; either right or wrong it is to be accepted. Clara had indicated an intention to have a birthday party, but Dr. Sotubo, her husband, disagrees. However, she is convinced by a friend to have the party elsewhere which turns into an embarrassing situation and a near tragedy. In the end, Clara is made to kneel before her husband to ask for forgiveness, in recognition of man's supremacy over woman.

The male characters in *The Sweet Trap*, by their negative portrayal of women, expose their propensity to suppress women. The women are pictured as being responsible for all that goes wrong in the play and seen as attracting the sexual harassment that comes their way. The women, by their actions, objectify themselves. In *The Sweet Trap,* Sofola fails to recognise the role of women as full and active participants in the development process of a home and society at large, rather she writes them as wives subjected to the importance of their husband. Male characters view and speak about the female characters in deprecating manner with the aim of subjugating and maintaining supremacy over them. An exploration of Sofola's *The Sweet Trap* shows that men explicitly (through verbal and non-verbal actions) and implicitly (through the demands of culture) discriminate against women or suppress gender equality / recognition and even discredit the women in diverse ways. This act of suppression cuts across age differences as represented by Salami (a youth), Sotubo and Oyegunle (middle aged men), and Jinadu (an elderly man).

Overview of Objectification Theory

Objectification theory provides an important framework for understanding, researching, and intervening to improve women's lives in a socio-cultural context that sexually defines, represents and equates a woman's worth with her physical structure and sexual function. Betty Friedan in *The Feminine Mystique* (1963: 15-16) expands on this:

> Over and over women heard in voices of tradition and of Freudian sophistication that they could not desire no greater destiny than to glory in their own femininity. Experts told them how to catch a man and keep him, how to breastfeed children and handle their toilet training, how to cope with sibling rivalry and adolescent rebellion; how to buy a dishwasher, bake bread, cook gourmet snail, and build a swimming pool with their own hands; how to dress, look, and act more feminine and make marriage more exciting, how to keep their husbands from dying

young and their sons from growing into delinquents. They were taught to pity the neurotic, unfeminine, unhappy women who wanted to be poets or physicists or presidents. They learned that truly feminine women do not want careers, higher education, political rights – the independence and the opportunities that the old-fashioned feminists fought for.

Objectification theory postulates that "women are sexually objectified and treated as an object to be valued for its use by the male gender" (Fredrickson and Roberts, 1997: 175). And according to Weskot (1986: 5), "objectification is the socially sanctioned right of all males to sexualise all females, regardless of age or status". While objectification may occur in many ways ranging from sexual violence to sexual evaluation, Kaschak (1992) observes that the most subtle and deniable way of objectification is enacted through gaze or visual inspection of the body. Objectification also occurs when a part of women's body is separated from her as a person and viewed as a mere instrument or regarded as those instruments that can represent her (see Bartky, 1990).

Objectification occurs in three related areas: in interpersonal and social encounter; visual media that depict interpersonal and social encounter; and in people's encounters with visual media that spotlight bodies and body parts and seamlessly align viewers with an implicit sexualizing gaze. Fredrickson and Roberts (1997: 176) explain that in interpersonal and social encounter, "looking at a person as an object merely for sexual pleasure or as an object for use is considered objectification involving beauty and appearance". They add that it also occurs in visual media that depict social and interpersonal encounters, supported by

Umiker-Sebeok (1981: 211) that "analyses from advertisements have shown that males are usually pictured looking directly at their female partners far more often that the reverse". Because sexual objectification has become so visible in viewer's day-to-day lives, it has become the most potent sector of objectification; this does not however, mean that the other kinds of objectification should not be resolved. Goh-Mah (2013: 71) used dichotomy and the differentiation between subject and object status in the simplest story lines to state that "...in society's dominant narrative, subject and object status is heavily gendered, with men granted subject status the vast majority of the time, and women severely objectified". This strengthens the idea that media's sexual objectification of women is something that stems from something much deeper than images seen daily.

Ford, Latour and Lundstrom (1991) replicated a 1977 study by Lundstrom and Sciglimpaglia that measured women's general perceptions of their portrayals in advertisements. Kilbourne (1999) relates that the result of the study proves that women are still critical of the way in which they are portrayed as sex objects in media advertising. These objectifying advertisements encourage men to be dominant and never take *no* for an answer, which creates problem such as low self-esteem for women. When a woman is portrayed merely as a thing, it dehumanises her which can lead to violence against the woman because a thing is much easier to manipulate and abuse than a person.

The third and perhaps the most insidious way in which objectifying gaze affects women is in people's encounter with visual media which highlights bodies and body parts and aligns viewers with sexualising gaze. Research on main stream films (Kuhn, 1985), visual arts (Berger, 1972) and music videos (Sommers-Flanagan, 1993) provide evidence that a woman's

114

body is targeted for sexual objectification more often than men's body. The society today is the most media saturated and media engaged in history. As media takes the centre stage in shaping the world's perception of itself, the individual struggles to maintain its unique identity. The individual absorbs the output of the media as the way of life and thus perceptions begin to form on certain genders, cultures and understandings. Kellner (2011) expresses that it is difficult to look at gender and not judge oneself in the process. One reason is that gender objectification is almost inseparable from everyday life. The positioning of men and women in society is controlled by their position in economy and social status and the power relations within these structures; it can be seen as an individual or public concern.

At a psychological level, perhaps the most profound effect of objectifying treatment is that it influences girls and women to adopt a peculiar view of self. In a related vein, a core social psychological view of self holds that an individual's sense of self is a social construction, reflecting the ways that other people view and treat that individual (Cooley, 1990).

The Sweet Trap

Zulu Sofola's *The Sweet Trap* explores the battle between the sexes, culture protection and misinterpretation of culture based on the conflict between Clara Sotubo, a well-educated young woman and her husband, Dr. Sotubo. The play underscores the imbalance of power between men and women in a Nigerian society during a transition to modernity.

The Sweet Trap opens with Clara receiving a feminist friend, Mrs Cecilia Ajala in her house. Mrs Ajala is in retreat from the celebration of Okebadan festival, a cultural activity which sparks contentious debate about how it has departed from the primary

115

reason for its establishment because of the gender abuse it has adopted. Dr. Sotubo had refused Clara celebrating her birthday anniversary which Clara still insists will go ahead, to the provocation of Sotubo. With support from Mrs Ajala, Mrs Okon and Mrs Oyegunle, Clara plans the birthday for Mrs Fatima Oyegunle's house. The hostess, whose husband Dr Oyegunle is as boorish as Sotubo, also suffers oppression from her husband but she has learnt to be defiant, to the consternation of the husband, despite her limited education; she dropped out of secondary school in the third year of study.

The birthday party takes place at the Oyegunle's residence, but it is disrupted by masquerades in the guise of Okebadan celebrants. Apart from the intruders, the guests find the rice dish unpalatable. Both events lead to the failure of the party. This does not augur well for the relationship between Mrs Oyegunle and Clara, who accuses the hostess of being a bad cook who also invited the masquerades to disrupt her birthday. At this point, Clara's uncle, Dr. Jinadu, intervenes; Mr. Ajala, the husband to one of the other women, confesses to having hired the masquerades to publicly disgrace his wife before starting divorce process. Dr. Jinadu condemns Mr Ajala for his act and advises that couples need not take extreme actions. He reconciles the families and forces Clara to humbly seek for forgiveness for defying her husband.

Okebadan and Female Objectification

Okebadan festival is celebrated annually to commemorate the founding of the city of Ibadan. Indigenes of Ibadan take part in the festival to re-enact the early days of the city, when there was general insecurity and limited resources. The symbol of the festival is known as Aboke, a man who dresses as a woman to perform rituals at the Okebadan shrine. Aboke dresses as a woman to depict the feminine nature of the spirit of Okebadan. During the festival, satiric songs that are sometimes vulgar, often mocking men and women, as well as nakedness and body parts, are sung. Most of the songs refer to the period of the extreme deprivation, when Ibadan was established; other songs refer to the military expertise of the Ibadan people. The festival is celebrated to foster peace and organization in the city. After the rituals, as related by Adesina (2013), the Aboke parades around the city, stopping to pay homage at the palaces of the chiefs and pray for peace and prosperity, and blessings for the community. The festival also memorializes the ancestors and heroes of Ibadan. In *The Sweet Trap* however, the Okebadan is portrayed as a festival for the ridiculing of female genitalia. Sofola uses this portrayal to criticise the festival as promoting negative images of women encouraged by the exclusively run local government to oppress women and assert male superiority. This is foregrounded at the beginning of the play the with the women agreeing on this point:

> **Clara**: But wasn't *Okebadan* a festival of fertility?
> **Mrs Ajala**: In a male-dominated society, fertility means femininity.
> **Clara**: So it is our sex that this festival ridicules?
> **Mrs Ajala**: Obviously. Have you ever seen the participants ridiculing male sex organs? Mark you; the attack on the sexes in this rowdy festival was not originally restricted to the female sex only. It was only in recent years when our women began to resist male domination and brutality that this festival degenerated into a rowdy display where men could take revenge for their bruised ego (p. 2).

This dialogue suggests fertility and common satiric intent as reasons for the establishment of the festival before it became an occasion for female objectification. Men obviously derive satisfaction from female objectification, as demonstrated when Salami relates how celebrants of the Okebadan festival molested a reverend sister under the guise of celebrating tradition. Salami found the flirtatious gestures amusing and a reminder to women of men supremacy He comments "...sometimes you girls need to be reminded of certain facts when you start to get out of control. Our forefathers understood women very well and so devised ways and means of keeping them in check..." (p. 29). The men optimise this opportunity to attack females for selfish reasons that are not related to the festival:

> **Salami**: There was a time when it was heavenly to be in the company of the ladies. Not anymore. If you dare raise an objection to what they've set their minds to, you will just have to run into fire. They won't fail to remind you of their degrees and diplomas.
>
> **Yetunde**: So that was why you disgraced Bisi Williams and her friends when they were shopping yesterday?
>
> **Salami**: Why not? They asked for it.
>
> **Dr. Sotubo**: What was that?
>
> **Yetunde**: The stupid boy went with Kunle and Ojo yesterday afternoon and created *Okebadan* scene right in the commercial heart of the city and disgraced our friends (p. 30).

In agreement with the notion of male dominance in the play, Dr. Sotubo, who is Salami's uncle, pretends to condemn the act to Yetunde but finds it amusing nonetheless. Even when Yetunde

118

relates the extent to which the boys went in ridiculing the girls, Dr. Sotubo refuses to condemn the act:

> **Bola**: Yes, Uncle, Ojo was dressed like a stupid woman...
>
> **Salami**: [*interrupts her*]: He was dressed like a lady of fashion, uncle. That's how you girls dress.
>
> **Yetunde**: It is only a crazy woman that would dress like that, uncle.
>
> **Dr. Sotubo**: [*to Bola*] go on, what did Ojo do?
>
> **Bola**: Ojo made such stupid jests flipping at Bisi's bust and backside and pulling Ngozi's wig and making funny pencils on their faces.
>
> **Yetunde**: Kunle painted Bisi with red lipstick from lip to ear [*Sotubo tries to prevent himself from laughing; Salami is actually chuckling*]. (p. 30).

This shows the extent of the problem; the men in the play seems to derive pleasure in demeaning the women, especially the enlightened and educated ones. There is an underlying vibe that the men would rather prefer to maintain dominance of the women, with women becoming silent and always pliant to the biddings of the men without questioning.

Female Representation in Sofola's *The Sweet Trap*

Nigerian female dramatists have been influenced by works of male dramatists and their portrayal of women in the society. The portrayals in the drama of the male writers have been majorly negative and suppressive. Therefore, in their writing, female dramatists view these characters in a different, more positive light. They redesign and elevate the status of female characters, and regard women with the same importance as men. However, the portrayal of women in Zulu Sofola's *The Sweet Trap* contrasts with the dramaturgy of other female dramatists. The

119

average Nigerian woman is strong and multi-talented and, according to Azunwo and Omovwiomo (2015: 15) "the physical strength of a man is equivalent to the psychological strength of a woman, thus, a woman is equivalent to the man". But Sofola holds a contrary view; in her writing, a woman's place is in being a subordinate as prescribed by tradition. On this stance, Sofola states that|:

> I feel the so-called modern educated women are ignorant of what the woman is in tradition and on top of that are arrogant. If they would only allow themselves to look they will find that they have no place either in the superstructure which came from Europe or in the tradition which they are rejecting (Fido, 1987: 59).

This attitude and reflection shape the dramaturgy of *The Sweet Trap*. The conflict in ideology between Clara and her husband represents Sofola's position on the clash between tradition and the changing times. At the end of the play, Sofola gives credence to her assertion by making Clara kneel and beg for forgiveness from her husband.

The character of Mrs. Jinadu represents the passive women in the society whom Ezenwanebe (2005) describes as being dependent on men and whose lives become conditioned by the patriarchal culture. She adds that they are "silent 'dumb' women who have no voice and hence dare not speak out their mind or air their voices, especially if those views are in opposition to those of the society" (Ezenwanebe, 2005: 79). These groups of women are completely subdued by the sanctity and supremacy of the gods or their surrogate cultural tradition, which is symbolized physically in the 'man head'. Mrs. Jinadu also represents the Conformist Woman whom Azunwo and Omovwiomo (2015: 14) describe as

120

"weak, gullible, uneducated woman; accepting whatever is given to them without giving a try to question cultural rites or any unfair treatment imposed on them". Mrs. Jinadu, though educated, fits in this category. The character expresses this position: "I am a university graduate myself, but my happiness is in what I can do to make my husband happy… if he says no and I see that he will be unhappy if I go against his will, I immediately abandon my plans" (p. 24). The woman has no life of her own; she is a machine programmed to serve a husband and do only those things he wants. She does not think for herself or consider her own needs.

On the contrary, Mrs. Ajala represents the active women whom Ezenwanebe (2005: 79) describes as "those who do not merely feel or express their feeling of oppression but courageously and confidently step out to act their feeling". Mrs. Ajala expresses this through her actions and dialogue in the play. For instance, she condemns male dominance and female objectification by protesting: "We have a right to our own lives as individuals, not as shadows of the male species […]. It is true that some of our educated men make their wives carry the dish on their heads while they eat from it. I know too that it will take centuries of education to remove the primitive stink in them but we are not sitting doing nothing… We are waging an all-out war for our sex" (p. 13).

Clara Sotubo on the other hand represents knowledgeable women. Her knowledge is explained as being a result of her education, exposure and enlightenment. She tries to use her knowledge as a tool to assert her rights when her husband instructs her not to celebrate her birthday anniversary. Instead of being submissive or loudly protesting, she suggests a more considerate approach to decision making in the family.

121

Dr. Sotubo: You don't mean you are still contemplating having that birthday anniversary

Clara: Yes, I am going ahead with it

Dr. Sotubo: After I have objected to it in clear terms?

Clara: Yes, I am proceeding with the party in spite of your objections.

Dr. Sotubo: And my decisions as to what should happen in my house carry no weight?

Clara: If the order is arrived at through a consensus of opinion by all parties concerned...

Dr. Sotubo: Wonderful! Has it come to the point where every order I give in this house, every position I take in this place, every instruction I give here must be contemptuously thrown through the window?

Clara: Did you think I would blindly accept orders from you without scrutinising them first? (p. 8).

While Clara calls for understanding between couples in reaching decisions, Dr Sotubo believes he is *the man* in the house and his definition of *being a man* is that he gives instructions that are to be followed without being questioned. His continuous use of first person singular pronoun on issues that concern the household emphasises his domineering tendency.

Female representation in *The Sweet Trap* is an unbalanced display of male chauvinism over females. The housewives go through traumatic experiences in the hands of their husbands who do not hesitate to inflict physical abuse at the slightest provocation; or engage in verbal abuses that define them as being of no value. In consideration of how the men treat their wives in the play, one is bound to ask: What happens to the phrase that we should treat others the way we want to be treated? What happens to the need of being humane? What happens to the cordiality that is supposed to exist between couple? The play ends without any of these questions being answered or any condemnation of the abuse suffered by the women.

Objectification Theory in *The Sweet Trap*

The Sweet Trap deals with the relevance of tradition in contemporary times and promotes cultural practices and their boundaries and limitations in human relationship. The play celebrates male prowess, wisdom, intelligence, wit, tact and boldness. It does not portray marriage as a union of mutual benefit and cooperation, understanding and sacrifice. The play is tied to the historical assertion that women have always been constructed as weak and inferior to men; socialized to be homemakers and supporters of men on the farm, for example. This point is clearly expressed by Dr. Sotubo, talking to his wife:

> Get it into your head once and for all that your university education does not raise you above the illiterate fish seller in the market. Your degree does not make the slightest difference. You are a woman and must be treated as a subordinate. Your wishes, your desires and your choices are subject to my pleasure and mood. Anything I say is law and unalterable. When I say something, whether you like it or not, clear? (p. 10).

The men in the play exhibit a domineering nature by wanting to have their ways all the time. They use authoritative tenses to put forward their opinions and brag about their power over the women. This concept of objectifying the women and seeking complete compliance from them influence their choice of partners. Dr. Oyegunle confesses her attraction to her wife, based on the need to control her pliant woman:

> **Dr. Oyegunle**: I married her because I believe at that time that an unspoilt village girl would make a better wife than these university rough-necks. I was sure at that time that a village class three pass would be better controlled than these citified society women.
>
> **Dr. Sotubo**: Well...
>
> **Dr. Oyegunle**: That village dunce has now become a burden... (pp. 21-22).

The continuous use of abusive terms by the men in the play also portrays their disrespect for the women. It shows how little the women are valued. The height of this is reached by Mr. Ajala who hires thugs pretending to be participants at the Okebadan festival to publicly disgrace his wife. In the play, Sofola conceive women as easily influenced and controlled and lacking discipline. The women are not empowered to take a stand and fight back. Clara is placed at the will of an insensitive and violent husband who disregards her feeling and reasoning. The element of objectification in the play is very glaring as Sofola addresses the way the men wield authority to suggest that the man is always right and does not need to consult with his wife in decisions concerning her or the family. This places the wife as an object, devoid of thought or feeling. Clara and Fatima are presented as punching bags for their husbands, thereby designating them as objects that can be battered and abused at the will of the men. From the way men are projected in the play, women are expected to be underdogs; qualification and other attainments notwithstanding.

The Sweet Trap addresses women's struggles against objectification but ends in an outright rejection and condemnation of women enlightenment. The men play key roles in plotting and executing the tragic end of Clara's party and abusive use of Okebadan to chastise women. Women desire to be seen and felt rather than only being heard, yet the forces working against their efforts are numerous. Staunch advocates for the preservation of culture in most cases are not ready to relax the rules to accommodate the demands of a changing world that recognizes the rights of individuals irrespective of gender. Women are not out to take the place of men, but request that human value not be measured in terms of gender; the relationship between men and women, should be more complimentary than competitive. On the contrary, in *The Sweet Trap*, the relationship between men and women is uncomplimentary. Even the elderly Dr. Jinadu declares a biased stance as he outrightly passes judgment on Clara and makes her kneel for her husband. He does not care about how Dr. Sotubo treats his wife but classifies Clara's defence mechanism as insubordination and traits of a child from a bad home, an attitude he would not support from her niece. Dr. Jinadu disregards Clara problems; yet, Dr. Sotubo whom he refers to as a gentleman uses abusive terms on Clara without any sanctions from him.

> **Dr. Sotubo**: ...I have tried everything I know of on that idiot... But I found that the more I tried to be reasonable the more senseless she became" (pp. 33-34).

One would ask if such words from Dr. Sotubo befit a gentleman as Dr. Jinadu indeed calls him. Also, what happens to the act of respect so often stressed in the play by the male folks? Could the

125

use of such words when relating an incident to an elderly person suggest respect?

Conclusion

Zulu Sofola underscores the imbalance of power between men and women as the Nigerian society attempts transition from tradition to modernity. Having encountered ideas of Western feminism that challenge traditional ideas about women's rights, Sofola creates women characters that seek to establish egalitarian relationships with their husbands. Like their husbands, most of the women are highly educated. However, their education and contributions to their households do not exempt them from their husbands' ridicule or attempts to have the wives submit to male oriented arbitrary decisions. Sofola critiques all ideologies and institutions that limit and impose hardships on women but ensures that traditional attitudes remain sacrosanct.

Sofola depicts traditional practices such as festivals to underscore how they can become perverted and be used to denigrate women, also highlighting the attitudes and tools that African women use to engage with oppression. Ultimately, she demonstrates that feminism in its pure form creates havoc and implies that however enlightened a woman may be, she should never forget her place as subordinate to men, living under the dictate and law of her husband. The play projects patriarchy and male egotism which socially constructs women as inferior to men. Sofola weaves through the image of the female as probable reason for the destruction of another and connects the play with the patriarchal nature of traditional societies, ignoring the wider vista of life requiring the woman's quota in building a home. She uses elements of myth and social belief to examine conflicts between traditionalism and modernism in which male supremacy persists. The play celebrates culture and agitates for its preservation. Sofola's *The Sweet Trap* does not treat the significant contribution of women to family and society as attempts to break historical, cultural and mythical barriers that prevent women from being properly represented in the society. This chapter suggests that there should be a fundamental change in gender relations to recognize the role of women as complementary partners in the process of development.

REFERENCES

Adesina, K. K. (2013). "*Okebadan*: A hill of historical significance", in *Vanguard*. Retrieved from https://www.vanguardngr.com/2013/06/Okebadan-a-hill-of-historical-significance/

Azunwo, E. E. and Omovwiomo, E. K. (2015). "Female dramatists, distinction and the Nigerian society: An examination of Zulu Sofola and Tess Onwueme's selected plays", in *Mgbakoigba Journal of African Studies*. 4, 1-18.

Bartky, S. L. (1990). *Feminity and domination: Studies in the phenomenology of oppression*. New York: Routledge.

Berger, J. (1972). *Ways of seeing*. London: Penguin.

Cooley, C. H. (1990). "Human nature and the social order", in Halberstadt, A. G. & Ellyson, S. L. (eds.), *Social psychology readings: A century of research*. New York: McGraw-Hill, pp. 61-67.

Ezenwanebe, O. (2005). "The Representation of women in Nigerian theatre: An issue in theatre development", in *Nigerian Theatre Journal*. Lagos: Society of Nigerian Theatre Artists.

Fido, E. S. (1987). "A question of realities: Zulu Sofola's *The Sweet Trap*", in *A Review of International English literature (ARIEL)*, 18(4), 53-66.

Friedan, B. (1963). *The feminine mystique.* New York: W.W. Norton & Company Inc.

Fredrickson, B. and Robert, T. (1997). "Objectification theory: Toward understanding women's lived experiences and mental health risks", in *Psychology of women quarterly.* 21, 173-206.

Ford, J. B., Latour, M. S., and Lundstrom, W. J. (1991). "Contemporary women's evaluation of female role portrayals in advertising", in *Journal of consumer marketing.* 8, 1 15-27.

Goh-Mah, J. (2013). "The objectification of women: It goes much further than sexy pictures", in *Huffpost Lifestyle.* https://www.huffingtonpost.co.uk/joy-goh-mah/objectification-women-sexy-pictures_b_3403251.html (retrieved 25 September 2017)

Ityavyar, D. and Obiajunwa, S. N. (1992). *The state and women in Nigeria.* Jos: University Press.

Kaschak, E. (1992). *Engendered lives: A new psychology of women's experience.* New York: Basic Books.

Kellner, D. (2011). "Cultural studies, multiculturalism, and media culture", in *Gender, race, and class in media: A critical reader.* 3, 7-18.

Kilbourne, J. (1999). *Deadly persuasion: Why women and girls must fight the addictive power of advertising.* New York, NY: The Free Press.

Kuhn, A. (1985). *The power of the image: Essays on representation and sexuality.* London: Routledge & Kegan Paul.

Sofola, Z. (1979). *The Sweet Trap.* Ibadan: University Press.

Sommers-Flanagan, R. (1993). "What's happening on music television? A gender-role content analysis", in *Sex Roles*.28, 754-753.

Umiker-Sebeok, J. (1981). "The seven ages of woman: A view from American magazine advertisements", in Mayo, C & N. M. Henley (eds.), *Gender and non-verbal behaviour*. New York: Springer-Verlag, pp. 209-252.

Weskot, M. (1986). *The Feminist Legacy of Karen Horney*. New Haven, CT: Yale University Press.

THE IMPLICATION OF FEMINISM FOR THE NIGERIAN FAMILY: AN X-RAY OF SOFOLA'S *THE SWEET TRAP* AND *WEDLOCK OF THE GODS*

Esther F. APATA

Introduction

Family is by far the most important primary group; the smallest social unit and may be regarded as the nucleus of the society. The family is a universal system that functions as the organizer and stabiliser of societal values and order. Murduck (1997: 8) sees family as "a social group whose members are related by ancestry, marriage or adoption and live together, co-operate economically and care for the young". Similarly, Mezieobi (1992: 171) sees family as "a social group in which there is sexually cohabiting men and women with possibly offspring or children resulting from the cohabitation". Mojekwu (1997: 25) equally notes that family is "a group of human beings of at least two adults of opposite sex and their children, if any, who are related by blood and have certain social responsibilities". It is a common factor in the definitions that three elements of a man, a woman and an offspring must exist before a family can be set up. Abraham (1966: 59) clarifies that "married couples without children, though bound by the strongest personal ties do not constitute a family, for such ties can conceivably exist among couples who are not married". According to him, what gives the family its character are children; for with children can can that intimate, personal relationship be established by which the family can perform its function of rearing, protecting and educating the children; transmitting to them the social values it has inherited, while also creating a special bound between all the members.

However, the high divorce rate in Nigeria today is evident in the changing profile of some Nigerian women as independent and empowered being which is leading to the breakdown of the family system. In view of this, Ezenwanebe (2008:32) expounds that "there is no development without change and drama as a representation of life embodies changes in the society". It is from this springboard that this chapter x-rays the impact of feminism on the Nigerian family system through the lenses of Zulu Sofola's thematic pre-occupation in *The Sweet Trap* and *Wedlock of the Gods*.

Gender and the Nigerian Family

Different explanations on the perceived differences between the female and the male gender have been put forward over the years. The focal point of the arguments centres on two very important but basic questions: To what degree does nature determine whether a human being is male or female? And to what degree are human lives shaped by their sexes?

The term gender captures the essence of these questions. Gender distinguishes between the biological and cultural dimensions of a being. Fatimah Mahmoud (1991: 141) echoes this when she explicates that "a person is not born female or male but becomes, through the influence of the society". This position articulates the fact that the distinction between the sexes is majorly a socio-cultural construct that metamorphosed into roles that are organized into patterns of behaviour based on the interpretation of the significance of sex. Virginia Sapiro (1988: 73) reiterates this perception further when she opines that "gender roles structure our choices and guides our behaviour in ways that are viewed as gender appropriate".

The Nigerian society according to Aina (1998: 6), "operates a system of social stratification and differentiation on the basis of sex, with clearly defined sex roles that are gender specified". This by extension means that traditionally, men do not participate in domestic work. They are the assigned head of the family who protects and provides for it. The man is vested with the power to make and take decision as the highest authority over every member of his household. The woman on the other hand functions in the family as the overseer of domestic chores. She keeps the house, processes and cooks all foods, and helps in planting and harvesting on the farm. She is also primarily responsible for the bearing and rearing of children from birth to adulthood.

Nonetheless, the gender and sex roles are not a biological category as much as a social construct that is subject to change, revision and multiple representations. These gender roles have been constructed through gradual, timely and orderly process of socially prescribed, family centred and community-based roles and responsibilities.

Gender scholars have identified culture as the underpinning factor that fundamentally militates against women's development in general terms. Over the years, the issues of feminism and gender equality have become integral in matters relating to the wellbeing of the society. Oyewumi (2014: 39) maintains that:

> Gender is best understood as an institution that establishes patterns of expectations for individuals (based on their body types) and orders the social process of everyday life, and its built into major

132

social organisations of the society, such as the economy, ideology, the family and politics.

Gender is therefore, a psychological, cultural and sociological concept. Oakley (1996: 13) on the other hand, believes that "gender roles are culturally rather than biologically produced. Whatever the biological differences between male and female, it is the culture of a society that exerts much influence in the creation of masculine and feminine behaviour".

From the foregoing, we can deduce that gender is socially constructed from the differences in the behaviour and role of the members that make up the society. This explains why the concept of gender is bordered beyond sex, or biological factors. While sex is a natural state which is a constant and universal, gender is variable depending on cultural and historical contexts.

The concept of gender for instance, which in common usage refers to the difference between men and women in social terms rather than biological, gained prominence in the 1960s when social scientists attempted to crystallize the social constructions of masculine and feminine relationships of individuals and groups. It was observed that gender relations have always been exploitative and oppressive especially where the female gender was concerned.

The questions however are: what do the male domineering focused roles spell for the modern contemporary Nigerian family? And with the emergence of more empowered, enlightened and educated Nigerian women, how can a balance be achieved between the two components of a family structure? These are some of the questions this chapter intends to highlight.

An Overview of *The Sweet Trap*

The Sweet Trap by Zulu Sofola centres around the conflict between Clara Dokubo, a well-educated young woman and her husband, a young professional. The play opens with Clara Sotubo receiving a feminist friend, Mrs. Ajala into her home after fleeing from a rowdy Okebadan festival scene. She intimates that the festival has degenerated in recent times into an attack on women for daring to resist male domination. Clara's husband however refutes this because, in his opinion, both sexes did not disagree on who should be the head of the family during the days of their forefathers since everyone knew their place and stay there. From the outset, the tensions in the play are laid out with the progression of the plot. Femi Sotubo refuses to allow Clara to have a birthday party. When she informs her friends, Mrs. Ajala, whose marriage is on the verge of collapse, and Mrs. Oyegunle, a semi-literate, they agree to go ahead with the party at the Oyegunle's house. The party takes place but is disrupted by Okebadan masqueraders. This strains the relationship between the women and the Jinadus, who represents an alternative kind of relationship in the play. To resolve the impasse, Clara is asked to kneel and apologize to her husband, a gesture of total submission and the re-enforcement of the male authority over the female.

Sofola portrays defiant women in the play as immature and irrational to prove a point that feminism, especially western radical feminism, is incompatible with the Nigerian family. Thus, she is more concerned with attacking the warfare between the modern Nigeria men and women. She insists on kindness and goodwill between couples. At the end of the play, Mrs. Jinadu leaves Femi with these words:

> **Mrs. Jinadu**: Please take care of her, things are going to be difficult for a while (p. 76).

Femi Sotubo seems worried and concerned for his wife. For the family, the cradle of human existence to survive, Sofola advocates mutual respect, love, peace, harmony and understanding in the home. This is the spirit behind the play where the Jinadu's bring peace to a fractured home and allow space for affection to reign. She sums it up in Mrs. Jinadu's lines below:

> **Mrs. Jinadu**: Yes, families have their fight, but the husband is the woman's most precious jewel and so is treated with tender care. So also is a man's wife the heart that keeps the blood pumping through a man's vein. Destroy this vein and the man is dead (p. 71).

To effectively achieve this, the playwright calls for the substance of status quo where the husband and the wife understand their place in the society. As Sotubo says:

> **Dr. Sotubo**: I believe that the battle of the sexes never existed... The roles were so clearly defined and each person so meticulously upheld the status quo that nothing like the confusion of roles was ever dreamt of, everyone knew his place and stayed there (p. 52).

Sofola's major pre-occupation in this context is the survival of the culture for a sustained good family life. She is therefore advocating for the total actualisation of the commitment a woman makes the altar, for the benefit of the family. She corroborates this view in the following lines:

> **Mrs. Jinadu**: …my happiness is in what I can do to make my husband happy.

> **Fatima**: Even if he says no to what you want very much?
>
> **Mrs. Jinadu**: Yes, if he says no and I see that he will be unhappy if I go against his will, I will immediately abandon my plans (p. 24).

The playwright's disillusion concerning the high level of divorce ratei n Nigeria, gender warfare and conflict in most homes today run through *The Sweet Trap*. She sees this trend as the refusal of couples to compromise and allow the family and tradition to survive alongside modern trends. And when Clara declares that she was leaving her husband, uncle Jinadu's spiky but disappointed response is:

> **Dr. Jinadu**: ...you have failed to behave like a child from a good home. I have hoped that by now, you would have settled for the better... (p.75).

However, a major fear of Sofola as expressed in *The Sweet Trap* is the changing profile of the Nigerian woman as it she serves as a major source of threat in most modern family. She is most critical of the modern educated woman who is not rooted in her tradition. Sofola tells women through the lines of Dr. Jinadu that education is not a "weapon with which to wreck a man's life" (p. 75). She expresses fears that if education in not tempered with tradition, it could cause untold harm to the future of families in Nigeria. From her perspective, the family comes before everything else and should be treasured at all cost. She speaks through her ideal model of ethical conduct in these lines:

> **Mrs. Jinadu**: It is not so. I am a university graduate myself, but my happiness is in what I can do to make my husband happy. (p.24)

136

The point here however is that there is an enormous generational gap between today's women and our traditional foremothers. This is because the family system has undergone series of changes alongside the nation's socio-political, economic and cultural development experiences. The pattern of change reveals the transformation motivated by changing values and prevalent economic conditions. Hence, today's women have also experienced certain levels of transformation and are much more independent, empowered, enlightened and confident with a critical mind of traditional obligations and practices. She resents not being treated like an adult who is capable of good judgment. Clara emphatically spells it out to her husband:

> **Dr. Sotubo**: Wonderful! Has it come to the point where every order I in this house, every position I take in this place, every instruction I give here must be contemptuously thrown through the window?
>
> **Clara**: Did you think I would blindly accept orders from you without scrutinizing them first?
>
> [...]
>
> **Clara**: You will find your instructions still standing if they can withstand the test of critical analysis, rational, diagnosis and intelligent scrutiny (p. 10)

Dr. Sotubo on the other hand believes that a woman is a woman no matter what and must be treated as a subordinate. In his views:

> **Dr. Sotubo**: ...your university education does not raise you above the illiterate fish seller in the market. Your degree does not make the slightest difference. You are a woman and must be treated as a subordinate. Your wishes and desires are

subject to my pleasure and mood. Anything I say
is law and unalterable…whether you like it or not
(p. 15).

This warfare between the modernist man and woman is what
Sofola sets out to address in *The Sweet Trap*. The men in the play
are not exonerated: Dr. Sotubo's stance that the home front is his
kingdom where his rule must not be questioned, where every
other person exists at his whims and caprices; Dr. Oyegunle's
idea of marriage as a forum to legitimize the control and
subjugations of the woman; and Mr. Ajala's attempt at teaching
his wife who refuses to conform to his will a lesson by setting a
trap that nearly destroys two families; are all condemned by the
playwright.

The clarion call for the full participation of women in the
decision making by Clara must be given full attention if the
family is to survive the ever-increasing tide of change. This is
because the nature of marriage and the family brings individuals
from different backgrounds together. Therefore, Sofola draws
attention to the fact that mutual respect, sacrifice and the
understanding of the human psyche are the keys to any healthy
relationship.

An Overview of *Wedlock of the Gods*

Wedlock of the Gods is a tragic drama which tells the story of a
young girl given away in marriage to a man whom she neither
knows nor loves. Her parents are in desperate need of the dowry
to cure her sick brother. When the new husband dies
unexpectedly, events take on a new twist. According to their
custom and tradition, the young girl is expected to mourn for
three months and then marry her dead husband's brother. The
young girl, exasperated, rebels in the face of custom and

138

tradition. In the play, Ogwoma goes against the tradition of her people in two important ways. First, she violates the taboo that forbids a woman mourning her husband's death from having a sexual relationship with another man. Secondly, she refuses to marry Okezie, her husband's brother to have a child for Adigwe, the deceased, as the customs demand. Ogwoma uses her husband's death as an opportunity to marry Uloko, her true lover, who could not afford the bride price with which her parents hoped to procure the medical treatment for her sick brother.

The conflicts of the play are multidimensional. First, there is the conflict between Ogwoma who wants to satisfy her desire for love and her parents who want her to sacrifice her heart's desire for her brother's sake. Then, there is the conflict between the traditional practice of arranged marriages and the modern liberalism of allowing a daughter to exercise her freedom of choice. In a patriarchal society, women are expected to be complacent and submissive, but Ogwoma is an independent and strong-willed soul and a threat to male overlordship, especially within the Nigerian family setup. Thirdly, there is the age-old conflict over who, between a man and a woman, is to be held responsible for a sex scandal. In Ogoli's view, a woman is invariably the guilty party because "a man goes to a woman. It is the woman who opens the door" (p. 10).

This play reacts to issues that plague the Nigerian family and the society at large. Sofola creates characters that struggle as an oppressed woman in a male dominated society. In *Wedlock of the Gods* not only is Ogwoma trying to break free from the imposition of her culture and tradition to marry the man she loves, she is also trying to break out of the male dominated society for self-determination. Sofola makes it very clear that the rules set by the Nigerian traditional society show that women have no hand in their own destiny because it is set and established by the man.

In addition, there are certain feminist moral lessons discernible in Zulu Sofola's *Wedlock of the gods*: the disadvantages of forced marriages; the evils of utilitarian bride prices; the ill-treatment of widows by relations of deceased husbands and the inappropriateness of the tradition of widows marrying from the family deceased family. The tragedy in the play is caused by the fact that Ogwoma is, in her own words, "tied like a goat and whipped along the road to a man (she) hated" despite having told her parents that she was in love with Uloko and as such is unwilling to marry Adigwe.

To Sofola, the tragedy of Ogwoma is the tragedy of many women in Nigeria, a tragedy of treating a human being like a mere commodity when the human being is, strong-willed, assertive and a feminist. Again, there is the tradition that demands that Ogwoma marry Okezie, Adigwe's brother. Radically feminist in spirit, her response is rebellious in the extreme: "I will be buried alive before I become Okezie's wife, she vows" (Act 1 Sc 2, p. 22). According to her, she has prayed the past three years for God to deliver her from the marriage (to Adigwe) and is now finally free (Act 1 Sc 1). Having complicated matters by getting pregnant for her lover Uloko during the three-month mourning period, her rational decision is to "run away before (her) condition shows" (Act 1 Sc1, p. 14). Unfortunately, before she can execute her plans, the bereaved mother, Odibei, naturally suspicious that her son had been poisoned by a reluctant and unfaithful wife, hypnotizes her and compels her to drink poison. Uloko there upon murders Odibei and commits suicide to join his lover in what would be a wedlock of the gods.

140

At the cultural level, Ogwoma would comes across as a cruel wife who denies her late husband the chance of having children raised in his memory. The final theme, to which the play tangentially refer, is the fact that it is not unusual for the relations of a deceased husband to maltreat and even disinherit the widow and her unfortunate offspring in the Nigerian family set up. This is the case with Ibekwe, Ogwoma's father. Ibekwe criticizes Okolie bitterly (in Act 2 Sc 1) of disallowing them from entry into their father's compound after his death.

Finally, the point must be made that Uloko's ending portrays the lovers as children of nature – lightning and thunder; riding in the clouds; wearing the stars as crowns; hidden away from an over-censorious society by Night. Even if we sympathize with them because the consummation of their true love has been unjustly hindered, we remain conscious of the fact that their sacrilegious acts have bred deep division in the community and within their families, in addition to bringing shame and psychological distress on family members. Ogoli, Uloko's mother, laments that she has become a laughing stock. This provokes Uloko to insult and accuse her of not having stood firmly by him when Ogwoma was to be given away to another man. Anwasia, Ogwoma's bosom friend, leaves the market when the gossip becomes too much to bear. "Nobody is on your side" (p. 22), she tells Ogwoma. Nneka, Ogwoma's mother says that the ground was difficult for her to walk on: "I cannot go to the market without hearing whispers; I cannot swallow food without being choked" (Act 2 Sc 2, p. 39). We are made to understand that what Ogwoma and Uloko has done is a forbidden act, an unprecedented abomination with an occult punishment of dying from a swelling disease with water leaking from everywhere, after which the corpses become a reject of all forests! No wonder, therefore, that Nneka says, "What you did has never

141

been done before" (Act 2 Sc 2, p. 37). Ogwoma's tentative postulation of the visionary's manifesto – "He sees what others don't see, and I will..." (p. 20) (referring to Uloko) – is halted by an indignant motherly slap and is not further developed anywhere else in the play. Calling the action "rash and hasty", Udo, a member of Ogwoma's family, tells Uloko: "You may be in love with Ogwoma, but there is a limit to what you can do" (p. 35). It is, therefore, as if Ogwoma's passions and acts are, to a large extent, social outrages thoughtlessly perpetrated by a spoilt child who could do anything she wanted to do in her childhood. Consequently, she grew up without cultivating the ethic that "a woman's honour lies in her name and her sense of shame" (p. 8).

Conclusion

The discussion and analysis of the play texts reveal the playwright's commitment not only to the course of women in Africa, but also the passion for the survival of the family. There is a synergy between the family and the society, as Sofola has shown in these two plays. This means that the changes in the nation's socio-economic, and cultural structures, and the changing profile of the Nigerian woman create a lot of pressure on the Nigerian family. The result and effect are the chaos and conflicts in most homes today, including problems of juvenile delinquency, drug abuse, cultism, prostitution and the high divorce rate in the country. Zulu Sofola in *The Sweet Trap* and *Wedlock of the Gods* suggests a recourse to tradition for answers. She also draws our attention to mutual respect, self-sacrifice and the understanding of the human psyche as strategy for a healthy family relationship.

Therefore, the modern Nigerian family must face the realities of our time. If it has become obvious that the woman's input is needed in all ramifications to achieve a well-rounded development world over, the family must also adopt this approach. This implies that every family must be open to dialogue and decisions should be arrived at through a consensus by all parties concerned. Every woman is to be allowed to fully participate in the process which affects her life and that of her children in the family and society at large.

REFERENCES

Abraham, M. (1996). *Genesis and family values*. California: Wadsworth Publishing Company.

Aina, I. O. (1988). "Women, culture and society", in Amadu, S., Adefanwa, O. (eds.), *Nigerian women and development*. Ibadan: Dokun Publishers.

Ezenwanebe, O. C. (2009). "The empowered woman in Ahmed Yerima's Drama", in *Creative Artist*: in *A Journal of Theatre and Media Studies*. Vol. 2. No 1, pp. 185-204.

Mahmoud, F. (1991). "African women and feminist school of thoughts", in Mohammed Sulaiman M. (eds), *Alternative Development Strategies for Africa*. Institute for African Alternatives.

Meziobi, K. (1992). *Themes in social studies education in Nigeria*. Owerri: Whyte and Whyte Publishers.

Mojekwu, V. (1997). *Laws of matrimony*. Ibadan: Heinemann

Murduck, G. P. (1997). *Concept of family*. New York: Oxford University Press.

Nwebo, E. (1967). *Eastern Nigerian family law*. Ibadan: University Press.

Sapiro, V. (1988). *Women in American society*. California: Zed Books.

Sofola, Z. (1973). *Wedlock of the Gods*. London: Evans Publishing Group.

Sofola, Z. (1977). *The Sweet Trap*. Ibadan: University Press.

INTERROGATING GENDER ISSUES IN TRACIE CHIMA UTOH-EZEAJUGH' S *EVERYDAY IS FOR THE THIEF*

Hairat B. YUSUF

Introduction

Women over the years have been in the spotlight in different spheres of life for positive and negative reasons. In instances, women encounter series of gender issues in political, economic, social, marital and religious platforms. Gender as a term refers to social roles assigned to men and women in the society, but the precise meaning of gender issues has generated a lot of controversies among intellectuals. The different feminist movements and theories have in a way restructure and recapture some misconceptions of women in the society. Therefore, gender issues articulate the politics of gender discrimination, expectation and liberation. Utoh-Ezeajugh's *Everyday is for the Thief* is a typical illustration of how men treat women as object of exploitation, deception, discrimination and use women's body as medium to satisfy their lustful desires.

An important factor of female writing is to direct readers attention to sensitive issues regarding women through creative use of plot, language, theme, characters, conflict, and resolution. Hence, every literary work could be given different interpretation. When one engages in critical analysis of female writer works, it can be supposed that many of them are from the feminism perceptive. Omolara Ogundipe-Leslie (2007: 547) submits that "feminism can be defined simplistically as any body of ideology and social philosophy about women since the word itself etymologically stems from the Latin word 'femina' meaning 'woman'..." Also, Pickering (1992: 41) describes feminist thinking as:

> Being a feminist means attempting to define one's self as a woman, rather than to accept definitions imposed from others. A woman's way of being in the world, whether the domestic, public, or professional world, is likely to be different from that of a man's. Being a feminist means believing that a woman's statements are as worth of being respected as those of a man's.

According to Ezenwanebe (2008: 187) "most African women writers agree that feminism is relevant to and necessary for African women, they recognize the need to pursue the emancipation of the African woman based on African ideals and through programs/actions that do not alienate her from African cultural and social realities". Methuselah (2010: 156) expresses that "female writers project women mainly as a prey and the men the predators. Mainly men… tend to make the women very frail and the man a monster that leaves the woman in helpless situations. Comparing this instance to real life, it is not all realistic". This quotation could be view as a very strong indictment on female writing. Further regarding female writing, Evwierhoma (2002), quoted in Ojediran (2010: 184), comments that "writing is also an avenue of empowerment of some sort of women since it enables the female writer to confront all forces threatening to silence her". This is however illustrated in Utoh-Ezeajugh's play as deceptions, deprivations, oppression and lust turn to be reality despite women's effort to have a happy home.

The existing and new feminism theories have in different ways express further the place of women in the society. Nwankwo (2009) opines that "feminism on the whole, has brought a lot of change to the lives of women. Feminism is no doubt good because it has to a large extent modified the earlier negative portraiture of femininity in literature. It has enlightened most African women to write about themselves…" Thus, anybody can be a feminist in as much as one refutes negative acts of deprivation and appreciates every human being regardless of their gender.

Gender issues in *Everyday is for the Thief*

Gender refers to the socially constructed roles, behaviours, activities, and attributes that a given society considers appropriate for men and women. Masculine and feminine are gender categories. Aspects of gender may vary greatly in the society. Some examples of gender characteristics in different society are: men have the liberty to smoke cigarettes in public but women smoking in some cultures are viewed as inappropriate; women do more chores than men at home; women are responsible for taking care of the family; and a host of other attitudes. Patriarchy is a social system in which the father or eldest male is head of the household, with authority over women and children. Defining patriarchy explains the reasons for the treatment of women through the ages and what it means to their future and success in life. Patriarchy not only explains how our society functions but how it controls women.

Dodson Gray (1982: 19) states that patriarchy is a culture "that is slanted so that men are valued a lot and women are valued less, or in which man's prestige is up, and woman's prestige is down". Steve Biko (1986) in Bamgbose (2012: 95) asserts that "one of the most fundamental aspects of our culture is the importance we attach to man. Ours has always been a man-centred society". With these views, women do not stand a chance of exploring their potential in the world. The existing roles of women still

147

operate in indigenous and contemporary society. Women are expected to get married, stay at home and take care of the children, while the men provide shelter. Similarly, men throughout history have always been perceived as strong, powerful, heroic beings. Men are depicted as fighters, providers, and of course first-class citizens, while woman on the other hand have always been perceived as faintly, weak, and unintelligent. To correct some of these misconceptions about women, several feminism theories have emerged. It is on this backdrop that *Everyday is for the Thief* is analysed.

Everyday is for the Thief mirrors a society where men turn out to deceive and exploit women of their bodies and belongings. The character of Chudi represents contemporary men who believe in playing relationship games with women, by promising marriage simply to achieve his lustful desires. Despite been showed genuine love by Amaka, he still lusts after other girls. Amaka represents the career woman who believes in nurturing relationships despite a busy career. Nonetheless, Chudi feels that, since she spends time working, she may be engaging in illicit affairs with her male colleagues. This is one of the commonest perceptions men have about career women. They instinctively tend to develop inferiority / superiority complex when dealing with women. They are also quick to blame the society and women for their predicaments. Some of the gender issues in the play are revealed in the characters and how they foster relationships with other characters:

Exploitation

This refers to the act of treating people unfairly to benefit from their efforts. The character of Chudi in the text describes how men take advantage of women, especially the career driven ones, by exploiting them emotionally and financially for lustful gain.

148

Also, the character of Oby represents the illiterate and unskilled women who are attracted to men without questioning their source of income; women who are easily lured with material things. Men take advantage of the women by making promises that they cannot fulfil, or by emotionally blackmailing women who are in a relationship with them. For instance, the following lines from the play, spoken by Chudi, expand on this:

> **Chudi**: Perhaps I need to search for a more desperate female to supply all my needs. Getting one is very simple you know. Just utter the magic words – I will marry you and believe me, if you are not careful, she will kill herself for you… (p. 89)
>
> […]
>
> **Chudi**: … It is now obvious why you refused to give me the five thousand naira I requested from you yesterday, even though you knew how badly I needed the money. (p. 92)
>
> […]
>
> **Chudi**: Make use of your connections to secure a job for me at Government House. After all, your uncle is the personal secretary to the state Governor. (p. 97).

The speeches are examples of the kind of encounters that career women experience in their relationships. The men, whether they are employed or not in employment, still prefer to depend of the women for material, financial and emotional needs. They also pretend to appear appealing to the women in their relationships. Many of the plays dealing with feminine or gender issues depict women as illiterates who are dependent on men but *Everyday is for the Thief* presents the obverse of the case. The play demonstrates that more relationships are focused on exploiting the women in several ways.

Deception

Women are victims of deceptions by men. Deception ranges from false statements to misleading claims where relevant information is deliberately omitted; it leads the receiver to infer false conclusions. In relationship, deception often leads to feelings of betrayal and distrust. Deception include lies, concealments, exaggerations, understatements, and equivocations. All these forms of deceptions are depicted in Chudi's character as it skilfully deceives ladies by promising them marriage.

> **Chudi**: …I have seen through you. My only regret is that I fell for your lies. I put all my trust in you. I made plans about our future. I planned to go and see your people next month… pay your dowry… perform the traditional marriage... the church wedding would have been planned for July… (p. 91)
>
> […]
>
> **Amaka**: I see everything is now as clear as day light. Promises here, promises there. And all the while, you laughed. How you must have laughed. How you must have had fun at my expense.
>
> **Chudi**: Please, Amaka, I will explain.
>
> **OBY**: Chudi, what is she talking about?
>
> **Amaka**:(*to OBY*) Deception, sister. That is what I am talking about. Can't you see? Deception has now its masterpiece. Three years of waste. Two abortions. Promises here, enticements there. I swallowed it all, hook, line and sinker. Thank you, sister, for coming round to open my eyes.

OBY: (*to Amaka*) Look here, I don't know what you are talking about. Chudi told me all about you. You are his colleague at work and you have been throwing yourself at him all this while. Unfortunately for you, Chudi is not that kind of a man: so go and pick on someone else. Your antics will not work on him. Leave my boyfriend alone or I will deal with you. (pp. 105-106).

It is clear from the above that Chudi has been deceiving both Amaka and Oby with promises of marriage, whilst playing one against the other. This is a kind of deception that Utoh-Ezeajugh uses this play to highlight about what goes on in the society.

False Accusation

This is also one of the gender issues that most women experience, explored by Utoh-Ezeajugh in the play. One of the reasons advanced by the playwright for men engaging in false accusation is inferiority complex. The playwright has been able to project this through most of Chudi's dialogues:

> **Chudi:** That is what you keep saying. (*turns round accusingly*) Look here, if you have another boyfriend, be bold and tell me. I can take it. I am a man.
>
> **Amaka:** (*astounded*) Chudi! What do you mean? How can you even talk like that?
>
> **Chudi:** Stop acting innocent. I know everything. I have carried out my investigations. I know about you and those doctors in the hospital. Your so called friends have so many tales to tell.
>
> [...]

151

Chudi: Well, you are the one who gave me cause to entertain doubts. After all, I had always trusted you. But the way you carry on these days... (*Shrugs*) I can't be sure... you spend more time in the hospital these days. And you are rather too friendly with those doctors. I have strong feelings for you. The thought of you with another man drives me crazy with envy (pp. 91- 95).

Freedom

For proper self-achievements and independent, women need to fight for freedom from the voices that have been silencing them. Achieving this aim requires a lot of efforts. Therefore, Utoh-Ezeajugh further demonstrates this through the dialogue of Amaka and Oby both of whom seem to have been under Chudi's masculine enchantment. Eventually realize they have been exploited and deceived in that relationship. To gain their freedom, the women confront Chudi with the truth, to which his response are anger and frustration; anger at being exposed, and frustration at not being able to continue exploiting and deceiving the women.

Chudi: ...Leave my stereo alone!

Amaka (*Panting*). You think I am a weakling because I have been your fool all these years. You will see the stuff I am made of today. I will show you what a woman can do to a man. I will reduce you to pieces of meat. If your father is able to recognize you after I finish with you, call me a bastard!

OBY: Chudi, you have used me and now you want to dump me. You will kill me first! (p. 110).

152

Oppression

In all forms, oppression is a distressing phenomenon, and women are mostly victims of oppression in the society. The consequences are myriad, including lack of self-awareness and lack of confidence in the women. It also includes a situation where the women have no recognition of their dignity due to tendencies that have already incapacitated their emotions and reasoning power. The tendencies may be a result of commitment to a relationship, psychological exploitation and emotional deceit. Oppression occurs in every facet of life. In *Everyday is for the Thief,* Chudi's oppresses the women, especially Amaka in a manner that is belittling as well as conferring irrationality and a sense of inferiority on the woman. Amaka is portrayed as a woman who reasoning ability cannot be equal to that of the man:

> **Chudi**: See your people for what?
> **Amaka**: (*giggles*) For the introduction ceremony. Why don't we do it this Easter?
> **Chudi**: How can you talk about an introduction ceremony when I do not have a job? What will I use to buy drinks? Will I use my urine?
> **Amaka**: But darling, I thought you said…
> **Chudi**:(*cuts in*) Do not remind me of what I said! I know what I said; I said I will marry you. What else do you want?

Conclusion

Gender issues are widespread in the society. This chapter tried to interrogate some gender issues existing because of the system of patriarchy in relationships, using Tracie Utoh-Ezeajugh's

Everyday is for the Thief. Feminism is a counter-hegemony discourse against patriarchy in other to create space for women in the male centred world. To buttress this, Macionis and Plummer (2005: 321) explain that feminism is "the advocacy of social equality for the sexes in opposition to patriarchy and sexism". Majority of women are suffering from disparities based on gender issues; the women know their rights, but they do not have the right channel to exercise these rights in a male dominated society, or opportunities to debate their experience. Tracie Utoh-Ezeajugh and other female writers have created artistic works to explore the exploitation and deceit of women by the men in the society, not only to raise awareness to the problems but to critically interrogate the issues with a view to providing further avenues for re-assessment of the issues.

REFERENCES

Bamgbose, G. (2012). "Modern African Poetry and the Issues of Gender: The Nigerian Literary Scene", in *Research on Humanities and Social Sciences*, 2(11), 94-105 (https://iiste.org/Journals/index.php/RHSS/article/view/3795; retrieved 11 August 2017.

Ezenwanebe, O. (2008). "The Empowered Women in Ahmed Yerima's Drama", in *The Creative Artist: A Journal of Theatre and Media Studies*, 2(1), pp. 185-204.

Gray, D. (1982). *Patriarchal as a Conceptual Trap.* Massachusetts: Round the Table Press.

Macionis, J. & Plummer, K. (2005). *Sociology: A Global Introduction.* Harlow: Pearson.

Methuselah, J. (2010). "Women Playwrights and Female Imaging in Nigerian Drama: An Overview", in *Journal of the Nigerian English Studies Association*.13(2), pp. 151-164.

Nwankwo, I. (2009). "Tenor of Humanism Re-reading Feminity in the Drama of Tracie Utoh-Ezeajugh", in *A Journal of Theatre and Media Studies*, 2(1). (http://www.ajol.info/index.php/cajtms/article/view/76632; retrieved 11 October 2017).

Ogundipe-Leslie, M. (2007). "Stiwanism: Feminism in an African Context", in Olaniyan, T & A. Quayson (eds.), *African literature: An Anthology of Criticism and Theory*. Malden: Blackwell Publishing, pp. 542-550.

Ojediran, O. (2010). "Dignity in Feminine Language: Exploring Julie Okoh's *In the Fullness of Time* and the Mannequins from Alice Walker's Womanist Perspective", in Dandaura, E. & A, Asigbo (eds.), *Theatre, Culture and Re-imaging Nigeria*. Nigeria: Society of Nigeria Theatre Artists, pp. 178-186.

Pickering, M. (1992). "A Feminist Vision for Clinical Education", in Dowling, S. (ed.), *Total Quality Supervision: Effecting Optimal Performance*. Houston TX: University of Houston, pp. 41-45.

Utoh-Ezeajugh, T. C. (2001). *Our Wives Have Gone Mad Again! And Other Plays*. Anambra: Valid Publishing Company.

THE WOMEN CAMPAIGN FOR CAPACITY BUILDING TOWARDS FEMININE FREEDOM IN THE SELECTED WORKS OF ONYEKA ONYEKUBA

Marian ADELOWO

Introduction

There is high rate of injustice against women despite the efforts of human rights movements, government and non-governmental organizations in protecting them. Women all over the world experience one form of threat or another; these are more prevalent on the African continent. Women are subjected to rape, domestic violence, childlessness, widowhood ordeals, human sacrifice, single motherhood, child marriage, forced marriage, and sexual harassment that come from spouses, families, places of work and religious organizations.

Through history, women are regarded as inferior to men as they have lesser legal rights, employment opportunities, family rights and suffer other various discriminations in some societies. Culturally and religiously, they are called weaker vessels that must acquiesce to men always, even at the point of death. Many women suffer from depression, fear, anxiety, sexual discomfort, drug abuse, and other psychological and physical trauma.

Childlessness is one the problems many women face with psychological pressures due to undue stigmatisation by in-law, putting blame on women. According to Rasak and Oladipo (2017: 45), a childless woman

> is constantly under stress, frustration and disappointment. She loses respect and may be ridiculed. She is always tensed and sorrowful.

156

However, a considerable number of people in the majority world have limited level of knowledge about the medical causes of infertility.

The cause could be medical or supernatural, although women are always blamed and traumatised. According to studies, the cause of childlessness could also be from a man, but a larger percentage of society approbates blames on women without scientific reason. Children are considered to be very important in marriages and many childless women believe having children will bring an end to all their predicaments. Conner (2014: 358) explains that "having children in common connects two individuals for the long-term. Yet, having a child in common alone does not guarantee the continuation of the intimate relationship". Many problems still come up in marriages even after having as many children as couples want, but women are mostly affected.

However, one of the solutions to problems women encounter is self-reliance. Most women have problem with finances and how to be self-reliant in all aspects. According to Swindle, Heller, Pescosolido, & Kikuzawa (2000 as cited in Kendall-Tackett, 2005: 46):

> There are many problems related to poverty. Women of lower socio-economic status tend to have fewer resources available and less support. They may live in neighbourhoods that are unsafe. They may worry about their children's safety at day care or school. They may face the constant worry about whether child support payments will arrive or not".

These unpleasant experiences linger for a lifetime and cause a series of health problems. It is expedient on women to equip themselves by breaking the usual financial bondage with which they are restricted in taking decisions. Financial weaknesses hinder a lot of women in fighting for freedom even when they are being traumatised.

Importantly, education is the bedrock of self-reliance, and it involves commitment and determination. According to Blanch, Filson and Penney (2012: 57),

> intellectual health comes with reading, having stimulating conversations, learning a new skill or language, doing crossword puzzles, exploring new areas of interest by taking classes, going to museums and libraries, or listening to lectures".

Due to some of the reasons already advanced, most Nigerian women find learning difficult, and that is why their problems persist. Education is a form of empowerment that illuminates and differentiates what is right from what is wrong. An educated woman will be enlightened on financial stability.

The Psychosocial Effect of Trauma on Women

The effect of trauma on women is not restricted to a particular society; it is a worldwide phenomenon. Caruth (1995 as cited in Kapla & Wang, 2008: 5) describes "trauma as a response, sometimes delayed, to an overwhelming event or set of events, which takes the form of repeated, intrusive hallucinations, dreams, thoughts or behaviours". Caruth adds that trauma is based on history which is man-made and self-inflicted and can only be understood through self-consciousness. Also, Frueh, Elhai and Kaloupek (2004) explain how trauma is caused by horrified events and experiences that people see to be distressing, such as the death of a loved one, being a subject of, or overhearing, inappropriate jokes in the work place and any number of experiences. All forms of violence, abuse, childlessness are also events that people do not have control over because they occur in a way that they do not have a choice than to accept them. According to Blanch et al., (2012: 2),

> Sometimes people aren't even aware that the challenges they face are related to trauma that occurred earlier in life. Trauma is unique to each individual—the most violent events are not always the events that have the deepest impact. Trauma can happen to anyone, but some groups are particularly vulnerable due to their circumstances, including women and children, people with disabilities, and people who are homeless or living in institutions.

Trauma causes problem that is beyond remedy in many cases, "and gives rise to feelings of intense fear, horror or helplessness" (Mezey, Bacchus, Bewley & White, 2005: 197). Different groups of people experience trauma in the society, but women and children are more vulnerable because they are more often and more commonly victims of sexual and domestic violence. According to a report by Adika, Agada, Bodise-Ere and Mey (2013: 81), "gender violence is perpetrated through fighting/beating of women, not allowing women to express their sexual desires in a man / woman relationship, not allowing women to handle leadership positions, and believing that women are supposed to serve men even when they are sick". Most of the victims delay in seeking help because they feel that nobody would believe them, and the reason is that the patriarchal African society does not positively value the opinions of women. Some are also afraid of talking to professionals for fear of stigmatisation. In addition, according to Akpoveta, 2008 as cited in Okorie, 2011: 176:

In Nigerian culture, the discrimination against women begins from the announcement of her birth which is usually followed with the sad exclamation, Ah a girl again! She is then dressed in pink cloth to identify her. Her toys are baby dolls to prepare her for motherhood and not womanhood. Many husbands on their part secretly or overtly express to have a male child as the first-born. Inadvertently the expectant woman would also wish for a male child as her first born in response to attitudes and behaviours that reinforce women's subordination.

Ashimolowo & Otufale, citing a United Nations Development Programme report, explains that the socio-economic development of a nation is usually affected by violence against women. "The greatest cause of violence against women is government tolerance and inaction. Its most significant consequence is fear, which inhibits women's social and political participation" (UNDP, 1997 as cited in Ashimolowo & Otufale, 2012: 104). Most societies are not aware of the above assertions that every case of violence against any woman affects her productivity, which subsequently directly affects the nation. Domestic chores are known to be solely carried out by women even when both husband and wife are employed in economic productivity. Women who are employed still do house chores alone, without any assistance from their male partners. This leads to increased stress and health problems, including high blood pressure (see Marco et al., 2000 as cited in Kendall-Tackett, 2005: 42). When a woman dies because of high blood pressure caused by any problem, the husband usually remarries.

A lot of married women go through series of trauma because they want to protect their status in the society or safeguard their marriage. "Many women in Africa do not support the idea of divorce in marriages, which make them to subscribe to any form of discrimination meted on them by their husbands and relatives" (Yarhere & Soola, 2008 as cited in Okorie, 2011:.176). They believe that women must stay with their children no matter what they are facing as a way of enduring their marriages.

One of the most prominent problems faced by many women throughout the world is childlessness, which has often cost the woman her live. It is believed that procreation maintains the continuity of a society and children are seen to be mandatory in marriages. Failure to have a child in marriage subjects those couples to pity and stigma. According to Owo (1994 as cited in Rasak & Oladipo, 2017: 43):

> Having many children makes one feel contented and important and also usually respected by others for not being childless. Marriage which fail to produce children often end in divorce. It is also described as the dissolution or abrogation of marriage. Psychologically, childless couples especially the women are always depressed about their condition; they always feel bad because most of the blames are levied against them. The pains suffered by childless couples attract sympathy.

Many causes have been traced to childlessness and most people in Nigeria attach it to witchcraft or as a punishment for evil deeds from the Supreme Being. However, Eisenberg (2011 as cited in Rasak & Oladipo 2017: 45) explains that it is mostly caused by low sperm count in men, problems with ovulation, damage to the uterus and blockage of fallopian tubes in women. In addition, excessive tobacco smoking and alcohol use, advanced age and Sexually Transmitted Diseases (STD) could create fertility problems in both men and women. In addition, according to Chelagat et al. (2017: 27),

> Many people believe that the infertile woman may have been promiscuous and may have aborted thus damaging their reproductive organs rendering them infertile. Infertile women are sometimes prevented from holding the babies of other women and told that they have no experience of taking care of any child. Infertile women have been denied (sic) to hold babies with the notion that they can kill other people's children in the manner that they have killed their own in the womb.

It is apparent from the above assertion that every cause of childlessness is attached to women and this causes psychosocial trauma in them which results in stigma, depression and anxiety. Rasak and Oladipo (2017: 44) add that "Nigerian men simply refuse to accept that they could be the problem and the women in their desperation from social pressures have been forced to help their men to bring in children from outside. Childlessness causes constant fights, misunderstanding and suspicion in the marriage. Sex becomes mechanical and unfulfilling".

Nigerian male writers who are expected to enlighten society and portray womenfolk from positive perspectives are the ones downgrading them in their texts. Femi Osofisan's *Midnight Hotel* portrays women as prostitutes; Wole Soyinka's *The Lion and the Jewel* sees women feeble and foolish; and Soyinka's *Dance of the Forest* also portrays Demoke as a prostitute. Generally, society sees women to be insignificant, weak, dependent, emotional and treats them as such. No wonder Nwanya and Ojemudia (2014: 52) observe that:

Rancour, bitterness and prejudices trail the first attempt to write about Nigerian women. This also points to the fact that patriarchal ideology is a dominant ethos in Nigerian society. As such, prejudices against women are extended to their writing. It is obvious now that issues concerning women and sex have never receive a good applaud in Nigerian Literature.

These are some of the reasons female writers are also coming up to negate and re-orientate society about womanhood, despite some hypercriticism against this movement.

Women and Self -Reliance: A Pathway to Freedom

It is believed in Africa that marriage takes everything from a woman, and everything about her belongs to the man. This assertion gives man control over the woman financially, sexually, physically and socially. However, studies have shown that the control is minimal when the woman is self-reliant. According to Conner (2014: 341),

> Economic independence can provide freedom from abuse. Yet, when it comes to economic independence, gender matters. Given the historical experience of women in the labour force and contemporary social factors, many women today continue to be financially dependent on their partners, women in abusive relationships in particular. Financial inequality is central to the female experience; it has shaped her role within the marital relationship, diminished her autonomy, influenced her place within the labour force, and nurtured her oppression.

Women empowerment is important and does not involve only financial aspect. A woman is expected to be empowered in all areas for her to be dependent. "The ultimate goal of women's empowerment is for women themselves to be the active agents of change in transforming gender relations" (Reeves & Baden, 2000: 35). Unfortunately, it is usually difficult for a woman in financial captivity within and beyond their immediate society.

According to Lower and Prout (2011 as cited in Conner, 2014: 357), "financial instability is one of the greatest reasons why, after gaining freedom, a woman has limited choices and may ultimately acquiesce to an abuser's attempts at reconciliation". A lot of organizations have been coming up to sensitize women about empowerment through education and how it will eradicate marital violence. In fact, education exposes, enlightens and advances people towards a better life which makes it a significant factor of human capacity building. In affirmation, Isa (2014: 36) highlights the functional essence of education in human and societal development:

> Education at all levels is the process through which individuals are made functional members of their society. It is also a process, through which the individual acquires knowledge, realizes his / her potentialities, and uses them for self-actualization and to be useful to others. For the woman however, she may not be so lucky to be that protected due to illiteracy, certain traditional beliefs, and poverty which may put her at high risk of abuse, neglect exploitation and violation of her right. Illiteracy and poverty are factors which put the woman at high risk of exploitation and violation of her right. Yet, she is

expected to be a good mother even in the face of these disadvantages.

It should be noted that the Blueprint on Women Education in Nigeria was launched in 1986, alongside the setting up of "Women Education Units" in Federal and State Ministries of Education. The population target of the unit is the school drop-outs, urban and rural women, teenagers, single mothers, women in purdah and literates who desire higher degrees. The aim of the programme, according to Isa (2014), is to ensure that women are educated at all levels with acquisition of vocational skills in hairdressing, dress making, cloth weaving, tie and dye, food processing and so on. The education and the skills acquired are to give them opportunity to be financially independent and at the same time earn them respects before their husbands and their family members.

Historically, Conner (2014: 350) informs that:

> The belief that females should be educated gained some acceptance despite its difficult beginnings. The education of women during the nineteenth century was based, in part, on the notion that children would benefit from the education of their mothers and that an educated man would be greatly benefited if his wife was educated as well.

This implies that the benefit of women education is for men and their children. This could be the reason some men want their wives to be educated but still make it mandatory for them to be at home to take care of the children without taking up employment. They see the education of women as a means of satisfying their own desires.

Looking at the advantage of women empowerment from another angle, Grupta and Shrivastava (2016: 14) see it as a way of building the nation because:

> Women who control their own income tent to have fewer children's, and fertility rates have shown to be inversely related to national income growth. Women are also more able - and generally more willing than male counterparts – to send the daughters as well as sons to school, even when they earn less than men. In turn, a woman's level of education affects her decision-making process when it comes to questions about contraception age of marriage, Fertility, child mortality, modern sector employment and earnings.

If Nigerian government really understood the implication of the above, there will be more steps and plans in empowering women for stable growth and development of the nation. In addition, Alonge et al (2014: 518) explains that:

> It is no gainsaying that women are catalysts for economic development of a nation. Many are into petty trading while some are into other economic activities. Apart from the buffer they provide, the tax on their activities, go a long way in improving the state of the economy. A sizeable number of women today are also holding key positions in banking industries, insurance companies, multi-national companies and host of others. Through these activities they help in strengthening the economy of their countries. Many women, particularly in the rural areas and villages are large scale farmers who specialize in planting food crops which help in achieving food security for the country.

It is unfortunate that women still face antagonism because of the view that an average empowered woman will subvert the social order of patriarchal and entrench matriarchal system of social relationship.

The Trauma of Childlessness in Onyeka Onyekuba's *Sons for my Son*

Onyeka Onyekuba's *Sons for my Son* explores the problem of childlessness in women and the control exercised by mothers-in-law. Women are usually blamed for any case of childlessness and mothers-in-law sometimes lead the victimisation and accusation of their daughters-in-law. Onyekuba, dramatizes the kind of financial, psychological and social trauma experienced by women in search of children.

Sons for my son is a story of Ndidi who is married for five years without a child. Her mother-in-law, Enyidie, gives her tough time and forcefully takes her to a traditional healer in search of a child against her wish. The dubious traditional healer, Ozoigbodu, tells Enyidie that Ndidi is *Ogbanje*[1] and her spirit husband prevents her from having a child for her earthly husband. Enyidie's belief in Ozoigbodu makes her to reject Ndidi's defence or explanation. What amazes Enyidie about the traditional healer is that he gives accurate details about her family; this makes Enyidie gullible to Ozoigbodu's soothsaying. Unknown to them, Ifediba, to whom they had revealed their details the previous market-day is Ozoigbodu's apprentice. Ozoigbodu gives them the list of sacrificial materials which will cost them a huge amount of money. Ndidi tries to convince her mother-in-law that Ozoigbodu is fake but she ignores her.

---

[1] It is believed among the Igbo people of Nigeria that Ogbanje is a person who is reborn after birth, or over and over again to the same parent.

Nneka, another friend of Ndidi, introduces her to a fraudulent pastor. The pastor collects money from Ndidi and attempts to engage in intercourse with her. With this play, Onyekuba depicts what women go through when they are in problem. According to Omoaregba et al. (2011 as cited in Lawali, 2015: 5), "infertile women who had previously sought help from a traditional or faith-based healer for infertility were more likely to experience probable psychological distress". This is exactly what happens to Ndidi, as she is forced to see a traditional healer and a pastor who are both fraudulent; this further traumatises the women.

As Ndidi goes from pillar to post, the husband, Obiefuna refuses to follow her even to the hospital for medical test because he believes the problem is not from him. Onyekuba points out how society believes that any case of childlessness should be traced to the woman.

Enyidie threatens to obtain another woman for her son. Apart from the patriarchal threat to women, women cause more problems for other women and this has eaten deep into the society. When the threat fails, Enyidie then tries to poison Ndidi to pave way for her son to marry another woman who will give birth to sons and daughters. At this time, she is not aware that Ndidi is pregnant and their childlessness is caused by Obiefuna's health problems. Although, "medical evidence shows that men and women usually have the same rates of infertility, yet African tradition continues to view infertility as a woman's fault" (Human Life Foundation, 2013 as cited in Lawali, 2015: 3). However, even when it is discovered that the fault is from the man, the woman still goes through trauma than the man.

From the analysis, any marriage without a child causes pain and agony to women, even when the husbands do not care at the initial stage. According to Rasak and Oladipo (2017: 47),

For most of history, childlessness has been regarded as great personal tragedy involving much emotional pain and grief, especially when it is resulted from failure to conceive or from the death of a child. With this greater diversity, once common pressures for childbearing have given way to greater social acceptance of remaining single or married without children. Before conception was well understood, childlessness was usually blamed on the woman and this added to the high level negative emotional and social effects of childlessness.

To corroborate the above, Ndidi is lost in her thoughts that she does not hear when someone knocks the door twice until the persons walks in and sits beside her.

> **NDIDI**: (*Startled*). Oh! It's you Nne
> Must you give people frights?
> **NNEKA**: I should ask you that question. I knocked twice there was no response. I would have gone back but the door was slightly ajar, so, I entered. I stood here watching you for more than five minutes… What is the matter? Are you alright? You look feeble. Worrying can only worsen your situation because anxiety, a sister to worry is not a friend to pregnancy. So, you better put your mind at rest so that when the baby enters, it will sit very comfortably. Anxiety and worry will not allow it to stay. Your mother gave birth to you, you in turn will give birth to your own baby (p.26).

In addition to the effect of worrying, Upkong and Orji, (2007 as cited in Lawali, 2015: 5) add that "psychological suffering is a significant and sometimes debilitating consequence of infertility in Nigeria. For instance, almost 50% of infertile women in Nigeria have been diagnosed with depression". This means that anxiety and depression cause more delay in giving birth. These women are depressed because of the pressure they get from their family members.

At the beginning of the scene, in her first appearance, Enyidie abuses Ndidi in the presence of Ifediba, who they meet for the first time.

> **ENYIDIE**: Does the road run about in the hot sun for fun? It is this barren woman here, for five years… (*Hisses. Indicates the five with her fingers.*) Five years is not five days my son. She has never conceived at all, not to talk of any miscarriage. I wonder if she is a woman at all (p. 8).

Enyidie comes around to pressurize Ndidi again for not having a child. She does not mind whether she has a visitor or not. Enyidie does not understand what Ndidi is experiencing psychologically.

> **NDIDI**: Mama welcome. How is everybody at home? (*No reply. She closes the door and follows Enyidie*) I hope that everything is alright in the village. (*No reply from Enyidie*). Mama, what is wrong?
>
> **ENYIDIE**: Ma what? Who is your mama? Don't mama me. Look at her mouth, (mimicking) "What is wrong?" So you don't know what is wrong eh? Now let me tell you, everything is wrong. Stop calling me mama, don't you know that you are also old enough to have grand-children, yet you

don't have a child. Since you don't want to be
called mama, stop calling me mama. You should
be ashamed of yourself (p. 65).

This is exactly what childless women go through in marriage and
it has been observed that mothers-in-law cause problem more
than any other member of the family. It is rampant in our society
that women have sex with other men outside, get pregnant and
assert that the children belong to their husbands. Most of them do
this to safeguard their marriages.

It is revealed by Nneka that Enyidie manages to give birth to her
only son on the seventh year of her marriage and she now has the
audacity to confront her daughter-in-law who is still in her fifth
year. Onyebuka does not reveal to us what happens to Enyidie in
her seven childless years, it is possible she also has the same
experience with her mother-in-law and other members of the
family and her actions may be a result of her trauma.

**The Significance of Self-Reliance in Onyeka Onyekuba's *Into
the World* and *Sons for my Sons***

Into the World is a drama of Tessy, a secondary school young
girl whose father enrols in boarding house after the death of her
mother. She suddenly becomes negligent and stops paying
attention to her studies. She has two classmates, Monique and
Mercy, who are intelligent and who advise her to be serious,
without success. Tessy prefers to associate with Patsy who is
equally unserious about her academics. After her secondary
school examinations, Tessy marries a businessman, Tim. She
lives an extravagant life because Tim gives her everything she
wants. Being a housewife, whose husband is rich, she has many
traders who bring clothes and jewelleries to her home. Tim
warns her about her extravagant spending and orders her not to
buy anything on credit again. He advises her to go back to school

so she could be self-reliant but she refuses. This also brings out the significance of education in self-reliance.

Onyekuba portrays Tessy as a woman who claims her right wrongly by blaming her husband for marrying her after her secondary school education and demands to be paid a certain amount of money every month. She also gives an ultimatum for either Janet their maid to leave the house or she would vacate her home, in agreement with the advice of her friends. When the husband refuses to sack the maid, Tessy packs out of the house, leaving her children in care of Janet.

After three years, Tessy's father and uncle come to reconcile Tessy with her husband. To their surprise, Tim reveals that he is getting married to Janet in a fortnight. He explains that Tessy left the children with him at home without a care, and he has decided to marry Janet who takes care of the family. He explains further how Janet passed her exams and is in gainful employment unlike Tessy who failed her secondary school examinations and spent her days in blissful unemployment. While they were together, Tessy caused a lot of problem for Tim and Janet and this is a cause of frustration for the husband. Later, Tessy is advised by her former classmates, Monique and Mercy, to empower herself by enrolling in a fashion design school. They explain further that men prefer women who are self-reliant, which is probably Tim's interest in Janet. Tessy enrols in a fashion designing school and reconciles with her husband.

Several media have been used to sensitise women about empowerment and this involves having the ability of controlling their affairs independently. Empowerment is not all about finances but refers to

Empowering women to be self-dependent by providing them asses to all the freedom and opportunities, which they were denied in the past only because of their being women. In the specific sense, women empowerment refers to enhancing their position in the power structure of society" (Gupta &Shrivastava, 2016: 14).

This implies that a woman must be able to stand on her own without the support of anyone; this will make her to be useful for herself and society. Onyekuba explains how some Nigerian women do not care about being self-reliant because of overdependence on their husbands. Tessy feels she can get whatever she wants with her beauty even if her husband refuses to meet her needs.

> **TESSY**: My sister, do I have an alternative? Since I don't have any handiwork, what else should I do except to eat, drink, sleep and watch movies.
>
> **MADAM KATE**: Are you complaining? You are one of the luckiest women in town. But you have to watch what you eat so as to maintain your fine shape before Tim starts looking elsewhere.
>
> **TESSY**: I don't need a reminder. (*She stands to show off*). Can't you see? I will win beauty contest any day. I can't joke with my beauty, it is the only asset and weapon I have (p. 25).

To negate what Tessy has in mind, Onyekuba uses Tim to let women know that a woman cannot use only her beauty to keep a man forever because there are other qualities a man looks for in a woman.

> **TIM**: Jane is now my wife. It was just to fulfil the formalities. She has all along been a wife to me

173

and a mother to my children who their biological mother abandoned. Tessy, I married you because I loved you. I gave you my heart, my love and my wealth but you trampled on them because (*mockingly*) you are beautiful. Did the Bible not say "...his position let another take". Jane has taken your position and she is better than you in all respects except in physical attraction. I prefer her inner beauty and resourcefulness to your hollow and ephemeral beauty... (p.58).

Madam Kate also points out an important issue that most women do not think about:

MADAM KATE: Look Tessy, things are getting more difficult every day. You don't know what will happen to his business tomorrow. Assuming something happens to him, God forbid, what would happen to you? How do you hope to survive? Meanwhile, you know little or nothing about his business. A more important factor is that you can never trust any man. He might get tired of you one day and things would change... (p. 26).

Onyekuba brings out three major points above; firstly, how will a woman who is not working cope with her children when the business of the husband collapses or when the man loses his job? Secondly, what if the bread winner of the family dies? What will happen to the wife and the children? This is a society where family members take over the property of a man when he dies, without minding how the woman and her children survive. Also, Onyekuba points out that women should not rely on a man because he could decide at any time to be polygamous. This is exactly what later happens between Tessy and Tim.

174

In addition, Onyekuba attributes lack of self-reliance by Ndidi in *Sons for my Son* as factor sustaining her agony. Ndidi is not financially independent and Enyidie uses this against her in most of the dialogues. Whatever she has, and any amount she spends belongs to her husband, even if it is monthly allowance, the money still belongs to him. There is virtually nothing she could claim as her personal property. It is not in drama that Ndidi loses her job or she is on leave, she is not just doing anything like Tessy in *Into the World.*

Generally, many men refuse to support their women financially if they are childless. "For instance, in Rwanda, the husbands of infertile women often refuse to buy food and clothes for her because she cannot give him a child in return; here, children are currency" (Dhont et al., 2011 as cited in Lawali, 2015: .27). When such women are not financially stable, how do you expect them to survive? They must endure any kind of torment they go through.

> **NDIDI**: ...I am not an *Ogbanje*. This is what all these *dibias* cling to make money. This has happened before, and we spent more than two thousand naira to no avail...
>
> **ENYIDIE**: Liar! What is your business with money, what we spend or what we do not spend? How much do you earn? Is it your money that is being spent? Is it not my son's money? (p. 22).

Ndidi has nothing to say to defend herself whenever Enyidie mentions money because the money belongs to her husband. There is another scene where Enyidie embarrasses her in the presence of her friend, Nneka when she tells her that her husband is not around.

ENYIDIE: …Yes, you always send him to go and accumulate wealth, while you sit here and enjoy. That is the only thing you know how to do. That is why you cannot get pregnant (p. 66).

What Onyekuba is pointing out is that if she is financially empowered, there will be a limit to the threats from her mother-in-law. Moreover, she will not even be at home with her to pressurise her. We also observe that in this kind of situation, when a woman is busy, it reduces her psychological problem because her mind is occupied with other things.

From the analysis of the two play texts, a married woman who has a child and the one who has no child are still financially dependent on their husbands. That means being self reliant in not dependent on having a child or not. Therefore, the two play texts from Onyekuba place great importance on self- reliance which is a solution to the problem of the women. They can only fight for and maintain their rights when they are self-reliant. Self- reliance will give a woman financial stamina to take decision without the help of a man.

Conclusion

Many organizations have been coming up to fight for the rights of women because of the challenges they go through in a patriarchal society like Nigeria. Most of them are going through problems that have affected them in every area and some are even dead because of the challenges they could not handle. Meanwhile, there are male critics who are against the freedom of Nigerian women, despite the effort of female Nigerian writers.

However, Onyekuba explains the importance of self-reliance in fighting for rights, even when there are problems like childlessness in the family. *Into the World* and *Sons for my Son*

176

expound that having a child or not having a child in marriage has nothing to do with self-reliance which brings financial strength. Tessy who has a child without being self-reliant has a problem with her husband who marries Janet because she is empowered. At the same time, Ndidi who is childless is also constantly having problem with her mother-in-law who points out her joblessness several times. This explains that financial dependence of a woman on a man causes more problems in marriage. Self-reliance of a woman earns her respect in the presence of her husband, in-laws and the whole society. This will also help a woman in controlling her affairs independently with minimal or no male hegemony.

It is also important to note that education is the foundation of independence. Education brings exposure that leads to freedom. In *Into the World*, Onyekuba portrays Janet, Monique and Mercy as successful women because of their level of education, unlike Tessy who refuses to go back to school after failing her secondary school exams. Onyekuba emphasises this because education with self-reliance teaches women their rights and how fight for it and maintain it.

REFERENCES

Adika, V.O., Agada, J. J., Bodise-Ere, K. and Mey, O. (2013). "Men's attitude and knowledge towards gender-based violence against women in Yenagoa, Bayelsa State", *Journal of Research Nursing and Midwifery*, 2(6), 77-83.

Alonge, H.O., Ige, M.A., and Osagiobare, E.O. (2014). "Women empowerment for self-reliance: Educational management strategies in Nigeria case", *Journal of Educational and Social Research*, 4(1), 517-524.

Ashimolowo, O. and Otufale, G. (2012). "Assessment of domestic violence among women in Ogun State, Nigeria", *Greener Journal of Social Sciences,* 2(3), 102-114.

Blanch, A. Filson, B., Penney, D .and Cave, C. (2012). Engaging women in trauma-informed peer support: A guide book. Philippines: National Center for Mental Health Services (https://www.nasmhpd.org/sites/default/files/PeerEngagementGuide_Color_REVISED_10_2012.pdf; retrieved on 17 August 2018).

Chelagat, D., Kerama, C.E., Morogo, W., Ayieko, M., and Maiko, R. K. (2017). "Infertility in Africa: A great manifestation of gender discrimination", *Journal of Humanities and Social Sciences*, 22(3), 27-29.

Conner, D. H. (2014). "Financial freedom: Women, money and domestic abuse", *Williams and Mary Journal of Women and Law*, 20(2), 339-397.

Frueh, C., Elhai, J. and Kaloupek, D. (2004). "Unresolved issues in the assessment of trauma exposure and post-traumatic reactions", in Gerald, M. (ed.), *Post traumatic stress disorder: Issues and controversies*. England: John Wiley & Sons Ltd.

Grupta, J. and Shrivastava, S. (2016). "Women empowerment in India-key for self-reliance and empowerment", *International of Research and Development*,5(4), 14-17.

Isa, A. (2014). "Integrating self-reliance education curriculum for purdah women in Northern Nigeria: A panacea for a lasting culture of peace", *Journal of Research &Method in Education*,4(6), 36-39.

Kaplan, E, and Wang, B. (2008). *Trauma and cinema: Cross cultural exploration*. Hong Kong: University Press.

Kendall-Tackett, K. (2005). "Caught in the middle: Stress in lives of young adult women", in K. Kendall-Tackett (ed.), *Handbook of women stress, and trauma.* New York: Brunner-Routledge, pp. 33-59.

Lawali, Y., (2015). *Psychosocial Experiences of women with infertility and their coping strategies in Zamfara state, Nigeria.* (Master's Dissertation), University of Ghana, Legon (http://ugspace.ug.edu.gh./bitstream/handle/123456789/21309/Ps ychosocial Experiences of Women with Infertility and their Coping Strategies in Zamfara State, Nigeria. - 2015.pdf; retrieved on 12 August 2018)

Mezey, G., Bacchus, L., Bewley, S. and White, S. (2005). "Domestic violence, lifetime trauma and psychological health of childbearing women", *International Journal of Obstetrics and Gynaecology,* 112, 197-204.

Nwanya, A. J and Ojemudia, C.C. (2014). "Gender and creativity: The contribution of Nigerian female writers", *Global Journal of Arts Humanities and Social Sciences,* 2(9), 50-62.

Okorie, N. (2011). "Development of journalism and Africa: Tackling violence against women", *Africana,* 5(2), 171-184.

Onyekuba, O. (2015). *Into the World.* Nigeria: Phyleom Publishers.

Onyekuba, O. (2015). *Sons for My Son.* Nigeria: Mercury Bright Press.

Rasak B. and Oladipo, P. (2017). "Childlessness and its socio-cultural implication on married couples within some selected Yoruba communities in south-west Nigeria", *International Journal of Innovative Social Sciences & Humanities Research 5(1),42-54*

PARADIGM SHIFT IN GENDER CONSTRUCT IN JULIE OKOH'S *EDEWEDE* AND *OUR WIFE FOREVER*

Rukayat ADEBIYI

> The "woman question" is not new, neither is it too old a topic to deserve our focus in times like these. Issues concerning the woman who writes and, therefore, speaks, as well as those concerning the one who is written about and so is spoken for, will for a long time to come remain pertinent in drama. (Evwierhoma, 2013: 15)

Introduction

The inauguration of feminism and feminist act in Nigeria can be traced back to pre-colonial era. Although, a written account of feminism and feminist ideology came to existence after Nigeria contact with the West, it will be wrong to affirm that "in Nigeria, the birth of feminism and feminist aesthetics cannot but be traced to the contact of Nigeria with other nations of the world, especially the West, where feminism already had strong roots" (Idegu, 2009: 80).

Long before contact with the West, Nigerian women had distinguished themselves as freedom fighters who fight injustice and oppression in the society. Some exceptional and extraordinary women of historical substance and developmental relevance in Nigeria include but are not limited to Oya (the powerful woman behind Sango), Yemoja (the river goddess of fertility), Inikpi (the brave daughter of the Igala Kingdom), Moremi (the courageous queen of Ile-Ife), Queen Amina of Zazzau, Madam Tinubu of Lagos, Hajiya Gambo Sawaba, and the Aba women of the Aba Women Tax Riot of 1929 fame.

Despite all effort by these women and women of this generation to proof their worth, the world we live in still presents limitation to the female. The female is faced with different oppressive situations at different phases in life. However, the marginalization, subjugation and victimization of women have being the concern of the Nigerian female writers. They have identified these issues and tend to proffer solutions through creative works. Feminist related issues propelled those women and concerned men who are activist and advocate of gender equality, opposition of violence against women to come up with several feminism theories to give credence to their feminist struggle. The condemnation of domestic violence against women has led to the coinage and postulations of various windows accessing female struggles. To Smith cited in Evwierhoma (2013: 19), feminism is "an ideology that attempts to improve the status of woman" in the society. Expatiating on Smith's view, Idegu (2009: 74) surmises that:

> A broad understanding of feminism includes women and men acting, speaking and writing on women's issues and rights and identifying social injustice in the status quo...feminism has remained the art, act and craft of overturning all, or most forms of gender inequality geared towards liberating women from subjugation and obtaining women rights; rights which they feel, or they are actually visibly denied by the male dominated societies.

Discrimination, inequality, marginalization, violence (mental, physical and domestic) are some of the problems women face across the board in their homes, offices, religious houses, political field and the society. The victimization faced by women in the contemporary Nigeria is not limited to social, economic, and political but it is extended and existing within womanhood. The limitations are seen in women against women violence, lack of univocal voice among women among others. Idegu (2009: 74) opines that "there are instances that women themselves constitute their own problem as women are simultaneously victims of themselves as well as victims of men and are upholders of society by acting as mirrors to men".

However, it is high time women eschewed limitations as they fight individually and collectively against the cancerous limitations affecting them. Gone are those days when female writers are docile and inactive about issues sensitive to women. The days when factors such as age, education, gender, sex, and marriage as well as critical attitude of male critics (see Ogundipe-Leslie, 1987; Okonjo and Ogunyemi, 1988; and Evwierhoma, 2013) used to be barriers to female empowerment. Today, Nigerian female writers such as Zulu Sofola, Omolara Ogundipe-Leslie, Irene Salami-Agunloye, Mabel Evwierhoma, Emmy Unuja Ideju, Tess-Onwueme, Stella Oyedepo, and Julie Okoh among others have realised this clarion call and have taken it upon themselves to correct the anomaly. Evwierhoma (2013: 24) avers that:

> The upsurge in female creativity arose out of the need for women to articulate themselves through the media of drama, prose, and poetry, so that their audiences would have a first-hand account of Nigerian feminine realities, which had hitherto been dominantly rendered by male writers.

The Nigerian female creative writers have woken up from their slumber to begin to put forth works that seek to redress gender construction by their male counterparts and misgiving female writers, correct the misrepresentation of women and their roles and ameliorate the prejudice done to female gender. In fact, female dramatists have made it a point of duty to "use the theatre as a vehicle for transformation and raising women's consciousness" (Emenike & Omovwiomo 2015: 3). Nigerian female writers through their creative work have sought to reposition the role of women in Nigeria, produce dramatic works that the women will readily identify with, challenge the relegation of women in patriarchy society and promote the elevation of women towards selfhood.

There is a need for women, according to Ruether (1988: 5) "to journey from patriarchal alienation to full selfhood in community" and this why the Nigerian female writers have made it a point of duty to fill the void of women empowerment and emancipation using different media. Amonyeze (2011: 22) surmises that:

> Playwrights have a knack, in voicing their personal opinions, to not only prick the public conscience but also act as vehicles for social, economic and political changes. Since their art is parasitic on the society, which they base the lives of their dramatic personas on, their creations end up revealing the major defects in the society's attitude towards burning existential issues.

The Nigerian female writers through their creative efforts have made concrete attempt to consciously or unconsciously, effect a radical transformation on Nigerian women from docile and passive to lucid and active. They advocate for an active and lucid woman who will be informed ideologically of her position and capability in the society. This is why most female creativities portray "women in diverse images and situations which affect them positively or adversely" and this portrayal has since become "a primary assignment for the female writer, especially the dramatist" (Evwierhoma, 2013: 31).

Relatively, Julie Okoh's plays, as observed by Horvat (cited in Ojediran 2012: 151-152) "do not only explore motherhood in relation to personal identity, but also expose the situation of female to female oppressive perception in upholding patriarchal culture". To this end, this paper analyses Julie Okoh's *Edewede* and *Our wife forever* with the intention of highlighting Julie Okoh's contributions towards the liberation and empowerment of women in patriarchal society.

Gender as a Socio-Cultural Construed Identity

Women are generally gullible to the fact that the society is the determinant of gender and so there is nothing to be done to change the social gender construction. Laws and customs, traditions and rules which have male faces have condition the mind of the women to see themselves as the weaker sex that should always be behind a successful man. Little wonder, Emenike & Omovwiomo (2015: 2) posit that:

> The perception of women has been that of weakened relevance and subordination tied to the miscellaneous oppressions they face in a world referred to as "a man's world". The world at large views the women as the weaker sex in different conditions – mental and physical disabilities.

The thinking that female is a weaker vessel that does not have the right to be independent is an identity that was given to women by culture and society to some extent. A dependent sex as given to women by society and culture has greatly influenced their thinking hence its contributions to the limitation and subjugation of women in Nigeria and Africa at large. The general assumption is that men are breadwinners and women are home makers, or that men are leaders and decision makers and women are followers and implementers of decisions. The society has printed a make-belief picture that has impacted men to see themselves as the stronger and superior being over women; it is either the men's way or no way. The society has constructed the female gender to be subservient to their male counterpart; a woman cannot be financially buoyant, professionally successful or be treated with respect despite that being successful does not have anything to do with gender. Women and their roles have been trivialized partly due to the way culture and society has affected the definition of their gender. Meanwhile, the difference that exists between a male and female is biological, the differences in the sex. The female understands this biological difference and has been working against its limitations, but the society keeps magnifying the minute biological differences to justify the injustice and suppression of women. Little wonder the paper presented by Naripokkho (NP) of Bangladesh[1] in 2001 for a training manual to eliminate all forms of discrimination against women declares an understanding that:

> Gender differences between men and women [to] represent socially constructed norms regarding the division of labour, and the distribution of power, responsibilities and rights between men and women, the basis for differentiation continues to be traced

---

[1] Naripokkho (NP) is a membership-based, women's activist organisation working for the advancement of women's rights and entitlements and building resistance against violence, discrimination and injustice. Since its founding in 1983, Naripokkho has conducted numerous activities related to Violence Against Women (VAW) in Bangladesh, which include campaigns, cultural events, training, research, lobbying and advocacy. For more information, see https://www.copasah.net/naripokkho.html.

back to biological difference. However, it is obvious that the biological differences between men and women are minimal and insignificant when compared with the similarities. Biological difference becomes magnified or exaggerated to represent an ideology of sex difference, which we refer to as the ideology of gender. It is used to justify unequal treatment of women and men (2001: 1).

Gender is a socially constructed identity of femininity and masculinity; the society construction of gender has painted a faulty image for the African woman. Perhaps, this is a reason for Ojediran (2012: 171) to express Gender as "a social construct which has incorporated the problem of identity, sexuality and the denial of autonomy that tends to make women voiceless in different societies". Social norms are so entrenched such that women who attempts to deviate from them get punished and any woman who go against these norms is often seen to participate at her own peril.

The Nigerian society has placed women at the receiving end of almost every situation of their life. They pay greatly for every mistake in all relationship be it courtship, marriage, or the death of their spouse. A woman is held responsible for every break in marriage ties, forcing women to stay in an unhappy marriage with daily physical and psychological violence rather than getting a divorce. The African society has privileged the patriarchal system to the extent that a woman does not have the right to anything or even choose the name she bears. Once a woman is married, it is expected she takes up her husband's name. A woman leaves her parents' house to start living with the man. The same society that discourages a woman from keeping her father's name after marriage encourages widowhood rite that is not acceptable to women, such as shroud maltreatment in a beautiful dress all in the name of ritual and rite of widowhood. The woman who had earlier taken a strange man's name in place of her father will be left to face hardship after the demise of the husband whose name she has taken.

The society the female find itself in a difficult situation. The society favours the male gender in all circumstances. The disgraceful, double standards women are subjected to in our society today is devastating and heart breaking. Several examples abound: it is only in a patriarchal community that a man is a genius for divorcing his wife in a day and dating other women in the next; six months later, he can marry a new woman if he chooses. Also, when a widowed man remarries quickly, he is labelled as someone who needs companionship and a woman to take care of his needs but when a widowed woman remarries after three years, she is labelled as a woman who obviously never loved her deceased husband in the first place.

In the male dominating community women find themselves, a man is free to love any woman of his choice and he is allowed to express this love to the woman while a woman who loves is expected to keep it within herself because if she is courageous enough to express such love to the man, she will be tagged immoral or indecent and such man might even begin to take advantage of her. A lady does not therefore have the right to choose and decide her marriage partner freely.

The Nigerian female writers and readers are quite aware of this pain and agony women experience; the female playwrights write plays that meet the yearning of the female readers who are looking for feminist characters to emulate, the characters that will lift their hope, the characters that depict the same things they experience. The feminine dramatists create characters that experience the same thing their reader does, and as such enables their reader to "perform a genuine as well as authentic act... the reader would see these characters in the reality of their own existence and empathize with them, especially when they are self-actualizing" (Evwierhoma, 2013: 34).

Paradigm Shift in Gender Construct

A radical shift from the societal construction of gender is an attempt to reconstruct and represent female gender status to abrogate the suffering of one sex at the advantage of another. This is because the social construction of gender has made women handicap not only socially but also economically and religiously. Naripokkho (2001: 2) states that:

> The normative underpinnings of sex difference lead to differences in the way responsibilities are allocated, resources are distributed, and rights are granted. Asymmetries or inequalities thus grow to represent "conflicts" of interest, so that challenges to the way social rules are constructed represent challenges to the entire organization of society.

To get the required result of gender equality at all spheres of life, women must be able to stand up and take risks to fight for their rights. The method employed by women to negotiate these changes varies depending on the ability or capacity of a woman to make changes to her life. Gone are those days when society is the determinant of woman's boundaries, when the decision on what a woman can do is made by society, culture and traditions. Today, women are quite sensible; they now stand up for what they believe in. However, the exploration of different methodologies through which women advocate for change in cultural beliefs, patriarchy attitudes and behaviour in Julie

188

Okoh's *Edewede and Our wife forever* is our main motive for this chapter. To analyse the paradigm shift in gender construct in the play, we shall discuss the factors limiting the enhancement of the female gender and character assertiveness of the playwrights to effect the needed changes in the gender construct. As we discuss and illuminate women's struggle for liberation and empowerment, we shall be drawing examples and illustrations from the play texts.

Edewede

Edewede, a play set in the hilly area of Otoedo land, dramatizes women's struggle to debunk the reasonableness for their oppression. In the play, Edewede the protagonist is faced with the difficulty of choosing either to save her matrimonial home or rescue other women from the deadly traditions of female circumcision. At the end, with the help of younger women, she negotiates for the change they want and win the battle against female circumcision.

Our Wife Forever

Our wife forever is a dramatization of the ordeal of widows in a typical African society where women are viewed as a property to be inherited after the demise of the husband. After the death of her husband, Victoria, a young educated woman in her mid-thirties, must undergo some traditional widowhood rites, which involve eating with dirty plates throughout the period of the rite, and not bathing or shaving any part of her body. To compound the situation, Thomas, her late husband's brother, insists that she married him if she still wishes to have access to her husband's property. Victoria, with the help of Felix, her late husband's friend files a case against Thomas for forceful insistence to take her as his possession and she wins.

Factors limiting the female gender in a patriarchal society

Nigerian female creative writers have come to identify some of the factors affecting the audibility, visibility, and sensibility of women in Nigeria to include but not limited to Self-limitation, Older women, Ignorance, and Cultural traditions and have begun to use their creative works to agitate against these, to promote the empowerment and emancipation of the female gender.

Self-limitation

The greatest limiting factor faced by most women is self-limitation. Most of the times, they believe going against the norms is a herculean task that they dare not attempt to accomplish. They prefer to fold their hands and allow things fall in place by itself. This limiting factor is seen in the character of the Otoedo women in *Edewede*. Edewede does not believe she can do anything to change the horrible situation facing women because she is just a woman that is only meant to carry out commands from men. The excerpt below illustrates Edewede helplessness of being a woman:

> **EDEWEDE**: I can do absolutely nothing. I am a helpless woman.
> **ERIALA**: Do you know what your problem is? Inferiority complex! Do you know what that means? (*WEDE shakes head negatively*) That means you under-value yourself. You see yourself as a cripple, incapable of doing anything for yourself. So, you wait for others to think for you, show you what to do and how to live. Are you really a cripple? Answer!
> **EDEWEDE**: Much worse than that. (p. 20)

The fear of the unknown has made many women unnecessarily submissive to their husbands. They endure all pains in silence in their matrimonial homes just to save a failing marriage. To question the authority of their husbands is considered a grave sin by the society. This factor has contributed to the inferiority complex in women such that any woman who tries to leave the confined status of misconstrued womanhood in the patriarchal society is tagged over ambitious.

Older Women

Most of the problems faced by women are engineered by their fellow women. The lack of united voice among women in the fight against female oppression, victimization and subjugation has been seen to be a major factor affecting their yearning freedom. Older women use wicked traditions to intimidate and oppress younger female. As reflected in *Edewede*, Ebikere, Edewede's mother-in-law, stands as the major obstacle for Edewede in achieving her goal of rescuing other women from the deadly tradition of circumcision. She (Ebikere) has been brain washed by the archaic tradition that she feels going against such tradition is a taboo that signifies bad omen.

> **EBIKERE**: Circumcision is part of our culture. My mother was circumcised. So also were her grandmothers, great grandmothers and great, great, great grandmothers. It is a rite that every woman in this land goes through. (p. 2)

In another scene of the play, Ebikere tries to manipulate her grandchild, Oseme into seeing the tradition as a rite worthy of participation. Against Edewede's condemnation, she (Ebikere) tries to cloth the tradition in fancy regalia.

EBIKERE: ...You will be brave my grandchild. Yes, you will be brave. Your bravery in the camp of circumcision will be the pride of your family and lineage. You are from a family of a brave warrior. Ah! The descendant of Edokparu, the Ogbomhagbesin, revered far and wide in Otoedo land for his military prowess. Oh yes, you will be brave. (p. 3).

The following excerpt also reflects Ebikere's determination to make Edewede fail in her quest to stop Oseme and other girls of the village from participating in the circumcision rite and rituals.

OSEME: I know, but I still can't see how circumcision and initiation are connected.

EBIKERE: Both of them are landmarks in the life of woman. The initiation ceremonies are the period of transition from girlhood to womanhood. My child, listen very carefully. The peanut is very delicate. It is the source of confusion, impurity and imperfection. (p. 5).

Older women feign ignorance of the harm done by the barbaric tradition of female circumcision; they are more interested in upholding cultural practices. All efforts to eradicate Female Genital Mutilation in Nigeria seem abortive as the custodians of culture see no harm in practicing the heinous act. In 2015, the former president of Nigeria signed a federal law banning Female Genital Mutilation, but this did not make some states stop the practice. Until July 2017 when the wife of the governor of Ebonyi State through her Family Succour and Upliftment Foundation with support from the United Nations Population Funds (UNFPA) staged an aggressive campaign against the

192

harmful practice of Female Genital Mutilation, the State still had the highest record of Female circumcision incidents in Nigeria.

Apart from the trauma and abuse a girl child experience during the process of cutting off the clitoris from her genitalia, they are also at high risk of suffering from infertility, infections, loss of sexual pleasure, haemorrhage, complications during childbirth which may lead to maternal death, and low self-esteem, among others.

A similar scenario where older women see themselves as custodian of traditions that are detrimental to their fellow woman can be seen in *Our wife forever.*

> **VICTORIA**: I didn't really mind shaving my hair. Though I could hardly control the tears that were streaming down my face, some women made it their duty to see that I cried at dawn, every day.
> **FELIX**: Why?
> **VICTORIA**: To let the villagers know that I was sorrowful. (p. 21).

These older women see it as a duty to uphold traditions under any circumstance. They find it difficult to give up the age-long traditions and as such see every new idea as a threat to the outdated traditions, without knowing they have become agent of oppression to other women. In the play, *Our wife forever*, Okoh shows how women are allowed in the society to participate in the discussion affecting society but their contribution is not rated highly. They have privilege to participate but have no power to effect changes.

> **VICTORIA**: That council is made up of men. And they are all biased against women.
> **THOMAS**: There are some women among them.

> **VICTORIA**: Those old women, do they participate in the discussions? All they do is concur with the men in whatever they decide. Then later, they ensure that the female members of the community comply unfailingly to the decisions. (p. 52).

Any woman who decides to take the risk of changing the status given to her by the society, culture and tradition ends up been the scapegoat. Such woman is tagged a stubborn woman who does not have respect for customs and traditions. The excerpt from *Edewede* below shows how Ebikere is trying to condemn Edewede for fighting for the betterment of women.

> **EBIKERE**: You have always been headstrong. Too stubborn! Humility means nothing to you. A well brought up woman should know her place and respect her limits. But you, oh no! You want to be in every place, have a word on every issue. You don't even know that you are only a wife in this house. And as such, your place is in the kitchen.
>
> **EBIKERE**: No doubt, you have very many qualities. See what they have done to my son. The child that I raised to be a man is now a woman.
>
> **EDEWEDE**: He is a man. A man who understands that a woman is not just an object to carry out commands, but a human being with feelings and emotions (pp. 7-8).

The promotion of female empowerment and emancipation will continue to be a dream yet to be actualized if the older women do not embrace modernity. The hindrance posed by them has gone a long way in supporting male in the oppression of female.

Cultural traditions

Culture has been identified as a people's way of life. It is their pattern of doing things, mode and manner of living and interacting together. Procter (1995: 334) sees culture as "the general customs and beliefs of a particular group of people at a particular time". Corroborating this is the postulation by Arinze-Umobi (2010: 56) that sees culture as a "people's distinguishing identity. Culture is an important aspect of human's life that binds a group of people together. It is a people's belief system, language, style of dress, art and so on".

The role culture and tradition play in the subjugation of women cannot be overemphasised. African culture has for a very long time been misogynist in nature. It is a major purveyor of female ill-treatment. Bature-Uzor (2014: 33) opines that "throughout the history of women emancipation, culture has always been presented as a barrier in the realization of its goals, of its tenets". In Africa, most of the cultural practices have social values that are mainly of utmost benefit to male. These values deprive the female of their freedom and right to empowerment. They are values that give women privilege but not power. Okoh shows in the two plays how culture has helped in encouraging the subjection of female to several inhuman ordeals in the name of traditions.

In the play, *Our wife forever*, by tradition it is expected that Victoria marries any of her late husband's brother if she still wants to have access to her late husband's property. The following excerpts are illustrations:

> **FELIX**: What about your in-laws?
> **VICTORIA**: I don't want to think about them.
> **FELIX**: Why not?
> **VICTORIA**: They are thorns in my flesh.
> **FELIX**: Are they bothering you again?

195

> VICTORIA: Will they ever stop? Just last month, they summoned me to the village for a family meeting.
>
> FELIX: What do they want this time?
>
> VICTORIA: They want me to marry one of Hector's brothers, now that I have completed the one-year mourning period (pp. 18-19).

Similarly, tradition and customs demand that she goes through horrible inhuman experience all for widowhood rite.

> FELIX: You've never really told me about your experience of widowhood rites. What exactly did they do to you?
>
> VICTORIA: Horrible, horrible things! Any time I remember them, I feel anger inside me. I feel sick. I feel like going to crush the head of all those who subjected me to those inhuman ordeals (p. 20).

Ignorance

The lack of knowledge about their rights has also been identified as one of the factors limiting women in their struggle for freedom against oppression and victimization. They feel everything done to them is right and do not question the inhuman ordeal they experience in the patriarchal society. To know the good is to do the good. If one does not know what is right, it might be difficult to do it and when your right is infringed, you won't be able to know. Ignorance is one of the major reasons why some women suffer in silence; they do not know their right and the limitations to the right.

The older women characters in *Edewede* are ignorant of the negative effects of circumcision on life. They feel it is the right thing to be done and that is why they keep on encouraging the younger generation to be involved in the act. Unfortunately, this menace not only claims lives of innocent souls, it instigates the silence and passive attitude of these women to issues affecting them. The following excerpt is an illustration:

> **EDEWEDE**: Our mothers practised circumcision because they know nothing about anything except for laws and taboos imposed on them. To stop them from thinking for themselves so that from childhood, they learn to be shy, silent and docile until they see themselves as objects for men's pleasure... (p. 35)

Way Forward: Empowering the Female Gender through Creative Works

Women are the only ones that can fight for right. They are the ones who go through the suffering and are in the best position to express the pain. The solution to most problems facing them is within their reach provided they are willing to search for these solutions. The first step to getting solutions to problem is realising that there is a problem and be ready to tackle the problem head-on. Ojediran (2012: 150) observes that:

> Women's ability to either speak out against or condone the unpleasantness of the unjust socio-cultural and historio-political issues associated with patriarchal society that does not allow them act on their own volition **is the determinant of their success in achieving the desired change they deserve** (*emphasis mine*).

To defy the reasonableness for women's oppression and victimization, one must be prepared to do what other women are scared to do, face the consequences of her actions and inactions "as those who speak out against are seen as rebels and those who obey are defined by their limitations" (Ojediran, 2012: 150). Mama Nurse in *Edewede* could not cope with the rigors that come with polygamy, so she takes the bold step to leave outside her husband's house.

Women have come to realise that for them to be able to effect the kind of change they desire, they must change certain things able themselves first. The shift from the docile and passive woman to the active and relevant woman has been seen to be mandatory. Achieving this goal will not be on a platter of gold but that of struggle and pains. Nothing good comes easily.

In view of the struggle to correct and replace the damaged identity of the female gender in a patriarchal society and ensure that the female gender is empowered in every sector of life, the Nigerian female dramatists have risen from their lethargy to begin using creative works to amend and correct the anomaly. To re-order the female gender steps, certain things must be in place. These include but not limited to Education, Supporting other women, determination and promotion of gender equality.

Education

Education is the key to understanding things perfectly. With education, the right information and knowledge will be acquired, and this will make women see things differently. One of the best ways to reshape and build a nation is to educate women. You educate a woman, you educate a nation. Edewede rightly put the importance of acquiring knowledge in the excerpt below:

> **EDEWEDE**: For the moment I know not. All I know is that knowledge is valuable. Through knowledge one learns to conduct oneself wisely in a world that is always in the process of becoming. (p. 42)

Supporting other females

This is one of the ways to achieving togetherness among women, univocal voice on issues affecting women among other necessities that will help enhance the empowerment and emancipation of women. Women supporting their fellow women breeds a solidarity spirit, as *together we negotiate, divided we fail*. The kind of scratch my back, I scratch your back syndrome Okoh advocates can be seen in the following excerpt of *Our wife forever*:

> **FAITH**: I make one like this for one madam. She like am well-well. So, I come make dis one for you
>
> **VICTORIA**: For me?
>
> **FAITH**: Yes. Na dis style dey reign now. Make you follow dem wear am too.
>
> **VICTORIA**: How thoughtful. How can I thank you enough?
>
> **FAITH**: Na me go thank you oh. Na who help me to pay for the sewing lesson? Na you! Na who buy de machine for me? Na you! Right from de day I enter your house, you take me like your pikin. Thank you, madam. Thank you. God go bless you well-well. (p. 67)

Similarly, we see in *Edewede* how the assistance Edewede earlier rendered to Ebun helps her get Ebun's support without stress and this lightens the burden of meeting with other women.

> **EDEWEDE**: It is very serious. I need your help.
>
> **EBUN**: You have it already. One good turn deserves another... (p. 28)

Determination

Every woman must be determined to fight against any form of oppression, intimidation, subjugation and victimization against her and other women. This determination is a personal conviction to achieving freedom from any limitation. The theme song in *Edewede* is a radical signal to women for them to stand up for their rights and claim whatsoever belongs to them. It is a ray of confidence to exercise the liberty to choose what they want, who they want to be, how they want to be addressed and what should be done to them. It indicates the essence of personal conviction and determination, because the right to choose what you want, how you want to be treated, belongs to you alone.

Aie ze n'oria	No one chooses for another
Ora to bo'ze	One chooses for oneself
Aie ze n'oria	No one chooses for another
Oria to bole ze	One chooses for oneself
Enó khole mhen tale	My personal convictions
Ole iyiarekhan	Shall dictate my course of action
Aie ze no, oria	No one chooses for another
Oria to bole ze	One chooses for oneself (p. vi)

Victoria's determination in *Our wife forever* to fight for what belongs to her without fear makes her victorious at the end of the day. Another example of how determination helps in empowering women and making them visible and at the same time audible can be seen in the character of Edewede. She realises the ripple effect of her long-time silence and decides to break it.

> EDEWEDE: … One day, I realised that I was merely an object, used by others. Then I said to myself "Edewede! You are human being. You must kill that fear in you. Kill it!" Mother-in-law, I have killed that fear implanted in me from

childhood. Now, I take my destiny in my hands. I speak on issues that concern me. And I follow my own advice. Nobody, I repeat, nobody can intimidate me again, not even you. Understand? (p. 7)

Promotion of Gender equality

Both genders have the right to equal hearing in the society. A gender balanced society breeds friendly and conducive atmosphere where both genders live in peace and harmony. Julie Okoh while playing her part as a member of the society uses her plays to advocate for gender equality. She puts strong and powerful words of admonition advocating for gender equality in the voice of a male character in her play, *Our wife forever*.

> **FELIX**: Where there is love, there is no master and slave but equal partners in the sea of life. (p. 89)

Also:

> **FELIX**: Honestly. For, I strongly believe that the breaking of the barriers between man and woman is the only ideal way to start the building of a new society. A society, where children shall be trained to appreciate the value of love, mutual respect and cooperation! (p. 89)

Similarly, Julie Okoh uses her play, *Edewede*, to explain through her character, Eriala, fondly know as Mama Nurse what God intended for both genders in terms of equality.

> **ERIALA**: Fairly well then. First of all you must know that God created man and woman in his own image.

201

If the image of God is one then man and woman
were created equals... (p. 37)

A fair and just society can only be achievable if the female
gender is accorded the same respect as their male counterparts.
The society will be a better place if women are given privilege
and power to express themselves and live freely without fear and
intimidation. Society should encourage fair and equal treatment
of women at all levels. Government intervention is also required
in achieving this. To facilitate gender equality, government
should formulate and ensure the implementation of policies that
would help showcase the productive capabilities of women.

Conclusion

In the two plays examined, women distinguished themselves as
agents of change, with commitment and dedication they advocate
for their right non-violently. Julie Okoh has used the two plays to
proof the indispensability of female gender in the advancement
of any society. She attempts to enlighten our society on the
damages some cultural practices have done and are still doing to
women as she condemns and advocates for change of some
obnoxious traditions that are against women in men dominating
society, a society where men with the support of older women
get away with inhuman oppression of women.

REFERENCES

Amonyeze, C. (2011). "A feminist inquiry into the rite of
transition and cultural divide in Femi Osofisan's *Women of
Owu*", *The Performer: Ilorin Journal of the Performing Arts*, 13:
22-34

Arinze-Umobi, S. O. (2010). "The bastardisation of culture and
value in the Nigerian home videos: A study of selected Nigerian
home videos", in Dandaura, E. D. & Asigbo, C. A. (eds.),

Theatre, culture, & re-imaging Nigeria. Nasarawa: Society of Nigeria Theatre Artists, pp. 56-63.

Azunwo, E. and Ejiro, K. (2015). "Female dramatists, distinction and the Nigerian society: An examination of Zulu Sofola and Tess Onwueme's select plays". Mgbakoigba: *Journal of African Studies*, 4 (1), pp. 1-18

Evwierhoma, M. (2013). "Female creativity and woman-centred ideologies: An overview", in *Female empowerment and dramatic creativity in Nigeria*. Lagos: Concept Publications Limited, pp. 15-66.

Horvat, K. (1999). *Cat on the Hot Tin Roof: Female Identity and Language in Plays of Five Contemporary Scottish Women Playwrights*. An Unpublished PhD Dissertation. Edinburgh: Queen Margaret University.

Idegu, E.U (2009). "Historical overview, global outlook, topical relevance and applicability of feminism", in Idegu, E.U (ed), *Feminist aesthetics and dramaturgy of Irene Salami-Agunloye*. Jos: Department of Theatre and Film Arts, University of Jos, pp. 73-87.

Naripokkho, B. (2001). "Social construction of gender" (Session 4). *Building Capacity for Change: Training Manual on the Convention on the Elimination of all Forms of discrimination against Women*. IWRAW Asia Pacific, pp. 1-6.

Ogundipe-Leslie, O. (1987). "The female writer and her commitment", *African Literature Today*. 15(1), pp. 5-13

Ojediran, O. (2012). "Language and psychology in the gendered psyche", *The Performer: Ilorin Journal of the Performing Arts*. 14: 171-180

Ojediran, O. (2012). *Speaking in an alien voice: A womanist comparison of the use of language by Scottish and West African female playwrights*. An unpublished Ph.D. Dissertation. Edinburgh: Queen Margaret University.

Ojo-Ade, F. (1983). "Female writers: Male critics", *African Literature Today*, 13(1); 159-179.

Okoh, J. (2006). *Edewede*. Port Harcourt: Pearl Publishers.

Okoh, J. (2010). *Our wife forever*. Ibadan: Kraft Books.

Okonjo, K. & Ogunyemi, C. (1988). "Women in Nigerian literature", in Ogunbiyi, Y (ed.), *Perspectives on Nigerian literature: 1700 to the present*. Lagos: Guardian Books Ltd., pp. 60-67.

Procter, P. (1995). *Cambridge International Dictionary of English*. Cape Town: Cambridge University Press.

Smith, H.L. (1990). *British feminism in the Twentieth Century*. London: Edward Edgar Publishing Ltd.

FEMININE ENERGIES: DRAMATIZING THE RISE AGAINST SUBSERVIENCE IN SELECTED PLAYS OF OSITA EZENWANEBE

Muftiat Oyindamola ADEYI

Introduction

Culture and traditions shape the structure of most African society. The communal nature of most of these African societies makes it easy for strict adherence to the norms and traditions of the society. Apart from being communal, most African societies are patriarchal in nature. This is not a case for the African society alone, as women throughout the globe have faced forms of oppression, subjugation, injustice, intimidation or marginalisation at specific points in time. The place of women in some societies seems to be non-existent, as they are seen as objects of recreation and sexual gratification purposes. As years pass, women are becoming more awakened and conscious of their being; they have realised that there is more to a woman than providing sexual satisfying for men. The agitation for equity and fair treatment of women has taken several media and dimensions, part of which are drama and theatre. While women continue to agitate for fairness, some male chauvinists see this clamour as a waste of time. In fact, some critics see this clamour for justice as disruption of societal peace and a way of "dewomanizing womanhood" (Udengwu 2009: 18). This is because they believe men are created to be the head while women should always be at their service. This patriarchal society thrive on male domination and expects the woman to go about her business without challenging her husband's or any male's authority after all "she is a mere woman who stoops to urinate" (Ezenwanebe 2013: 29).

Several scholars across the ball have come up with different names for the women's struggle for equity, depending on the region or method she has decided to adopt; names including Feminism, Womanism, Motherism, and Stiwanism. This is to buttress the fact that the females are disadvantaged against their male counterparts. "Feminist theatre is committed to raising feminist consciousness with political implications since the dramatist recognises that theatre can be used to resist or support the status-quo" Ebo (2009: 394).

The Womanist theatre of Osita Ezenwanebe is examined through two of her plays *Adaugo* and *Shadows on Arrival,* where we understand how women in both traditional and modern contemporary societies strive to be heard and rise against subjugation in their own unique ways.

Theoretical framework

This chapter is an extrinsic analysis of Osita Ezenwanebe's plays, *Adaugo* and *Shadows on Arrival*. The texts are analysed in line with the womanist theory. Womanism, which is a brand of Feminism, is believed to be the most suitable theory for black women struggles. It takes a holistic view of a situation and analyses it as a communal problem, and not just the cross of the individual involved only. It is culture oriented and keeps in check the family ideal. The term Womanism is credited to American novelist Alice Walker in her collection of essays titled, *In Search of Our Mothers' Gardens* published in 1983.The womanist movement for Walker understands the black womanhood better; feminism on the other hand is more suitable for middle class white women.

Walker (1984: 100) posits that "Womanist encompasses feminist as it is defined… it has a strong root in black women's culture".

206

She contends further that, an advantage of using Womanism to feminism is "because it is from my own culture, I needn't preface it with the word 'black' (an awkward necessity and a problem I have with the word feminist)". With reference to Alice Walker's explanation, we can infer that the term Womanism gives room for the black womanhood to celebrate their colour and culture and express their struggles in ways pertinent to them. Womanism therefore stands for the integration and wholeness of the community without being a separatist. It celebrates black roots, examines women's social roles, emotions and the ideals of life, as well as redefining the African woman's culture. Womanism believes in the partnership with men.

Reflections on Literature

Feminist discourse in Africa has continued to take different forms and dimensions. It is no longer secret that African women have found their voice under patriarchy and are now demanding for a just and fair treatment. The feminist / womanist movement is a premise for women to air their struggle and choose suitable forms that suit their clamour for fairness. Therefore, attempts to pin feminism to one basic definition may be futile, as the level of struggle connotes different things to various people. The reason may not be unconnected to the opinion of Idegu (2009: 74) that:

> Defining feminism can be challenging and problematic because of its universality and of course, topicality in concept and practice... simply put, from about the 18th century till date, feminism has remained the art, act, and craft of overturning all, or most of gender inequality geared towards liberating women from subjugation and obtaining women rights; rights which they feel, or they are actually visibly denied by the male dominated societies.

The above highlights the reason for feminism. Since the movement is a global phenomenon, there are diverse approaches to the movement dictated by cultural realities of one region to another. Therefore:

> There is hardly a generally accepted concept even amongst the feminist as each group aligns and readjusts to concepts like African Feminism, Womanism, Femalism, African Feminism, and yet others in their multiplicity of agitations… rather than see the varying concepts and practice of feminism bearing different names as a minus for feminist aesthetics, I see it as an added advantage of the dynamism of the principle and objectives of feminism (Idegu 2009: 81-82).

The need to be heard and to tell their stories by themselves is why we have several female writers / dramatists. It is believed that a male writer may biased in representing women's issues. The make writer is writing outside the self and has no personal experience of the issues. Women writers are more likely to pay attention to female characters than the men do, which allows us to understand Sherry's, (1989: 2-3) submission that:

> Of course, relatively few writers confine themselves entirely to writing about the experiences of one sex only, and have often written about women, just as most women writers include both sexes in their fiction and drama…however, in these works written by men, and the women character are almost always seen primarily in relation to men, and they are usually of interest largely in terms of their romantic and sexual relationships.

To support Sherry's submission, Azuike (2011: 47) adds that:

> Mythical stereotypes about women abound and these stereotypes have continued to support male dominance and the general devaluation of women. These mystical stereotypes have also included the views that recognize women only in terms of sexuality and reproduction. One of these views is that the woman is "the beast of burden", and so must bear the greater burden of responsibility, for propagation and for nurturance.

It is only natural that women tell their stories better, and re write themselves in a fairer way. Some women face a lot of oppression and subjugation without even knowing they are being oppressed, while others have chosen to be silent and docile, because not challenging the oppressor is what they have been taught and fed all their lives. For instance:

> Women are often depicted in the media in a stereo typical and derogatory manner and her hardly shown in their professional capacities, except in their domestic sphere considered to be their sphere of influence. The commodification of women's body in media advert has exacerbated the already battered image of women in the society (Alao & Ogundeji 2014: 160).

To protect the present and coming generation from further inequalities, and to exhibit their inner strength "women in many African societies have risen as redeemers to rescue a male dominated society" (Salami-Agunloye 2011: 87). Even though, there is an ongoing discourse on women and representation, Aliyu (2012: 61) argues that:

For a continent such as Africa which promotes cultural practices which are believed to enforce women's subservience, the complimentary roles expected from women to their male counterparts in terms of providing a stable home front, supportive companionship and even economic support underscore elements of discrimination between the sexes...

[...]

Practices such as the demand and payment of large bride-prices on girls, limiting access to Western education for the girl-child and restricting women from engaging in key economic activities capable of propelling them into economic independence are some practices which continue to subjugate the African woman and promote male dominance.

In the same vein, Ojediran (2014: 172) believes that "women writers have always neglected the role of women in democratic politics; rather they often discuss women's positions in socio-cultural, economic and traditional settings". It is, therefore, the crux of feminists to ensure that while agitating against subservience of women, erroneous and/or under representation of these women should be avoided.

Feminist Rise against Subservience in Osita Ezenwanebe's *Shadows on Arrival*

Shadows on Arrival by Osita Ezenwanebe celebrates the strength of the traditional African woman. The play shows how Egoyinbo, the central character in the play, uses her resilience as a tool to liberate her family from the dangerous conservativism of the patriarchal society represented in the office and person of the chief priest; to resist oppressive culture against women; and

210

to embrace change. The setting is Umueze village, where Ezemuo, the corrupt chief priest of the village, decides to punish Egoyinbo – a mere woman – for denying his sexual advances. To deal with the situation and make Egoyinbo realise his importance, he exploits his spiritual office to confine Egoyinbo's only child to the forest of the gods as an *ogbanje*[1]. Egoyinbo's non-violent resilience, delivers her child, Agbomma, from defilement and makes her conservative husband Agwudo realise the lies of Ezemuo. Egoyinbo uses her feminine power and strength to combat injustice, free her household from oppression and consequently makes Ezemuo pay dearly for his corruption and exploitation of a spiritual office.

Shadows on Arrival explores the strength of women in traditional Igbo society. It depicts how illiterate women in the traditional society are viewed and treated by their community. It shows how upholders of tradition misuse power and how customs are revered. Women are only present in the society for procreation and domestic work with no viable position in decision making. While many patriarchal societies believe that women are supposed to be 'seen and not heard', in Umueze community, women are not supposed to be seen and heard, and ultimately are not allowed to have a voice. Therefore, Egoyibo's friends see the likes of Chika who "ran to the god of the strangers". (p. 13) where she gains a voice to say no, to killing her albino child, as inevitably mad.

It is expected that a woman's house whether owned by her husband or herself is also her house and vice-versa. Therefore, it is only natural to use words like 'I am going home' or 'I am going to my house' but in Umueze community, women use

---

[1] Ogbanje is a person who is reborn after birth to the same parent; a belief amongst Igbo people.

expressions like "I am going back to my husband's house" (p. 11). The above lines throw more light on the belief that most women like Egoyibo in the community, are their husband's property, and are never going to challenge their husband's authority.

The excessive display of machismo by Agwudo towards Egoyibo mirrors how men see women as subordinates who do not know how to act except when they are told what to do by their husbands. This plays out in Agwudo's sarcasm to his wife.

> **AGWUDO**: *(Thunders.)* you were still discussing? What were you women discussing? Were you discussing how to fight Umuno town and recover the stolen *Ofo* staff of Umuedo town! Or, were you discussing how to crown the next *Igwe* of our town, Umueze! *Oho o*, maybe you are planning how to send away the white invaders from our land. Tell me what is meaningful that mere women who stoop to urinate, can possibly be discussing that made you stay on the major pathway to *Agbala Oha* when you heard the sacred *ekwe*? Egoyibo! Egoyibo! It is a person who eats a rotten nut that releases a foul fart. (p. 15)

The above statement makes it easy to understand that Agwudo ignorantly believes women are useful for gossips and no other productive things. Agwudo finds it disturbing that they – mere women – dare peep at titled men. He reminds her that they damn the consequence of being accused of eavesdropping on the titled men meeting.

212

Although, we find Agwudo, warmer with his *ogbanje* girl-child. He still has some conviction that she would have been better off if she were to be a man, when he wonders "why the gods made you a woman; you are supposed to be a man but the gods know better" (p. 16). This we believe is part of the reason Agwudo trains the girl in school as evidently captured in this statement:

> **AGBOMMA**: That's why you sent me to the white man's school even when your friends were against it. Remember what Ichie Dike told you; that it is useless training a girl because she will marry and carry everything to her husband's house. He also said em...em..., remind me that thing he said papa; yes, that training a girl is like building a house on another man's land (p. 38).

Agbomma is the future of women in the society; she indicates her interest to go to school and is surprisingly supported by her father against the stance of the community and council of elders. This may be because she is the only child, "you know as an only child, she is more than a woman to me and our people, because she will stay back in my compound to populate my homestead so that my lineage will not close down" (p. 52).

The strength of a woman is unimaginable, part of which is her ability to nurture life in her. It is no surprise then that a mother would go to any length to protect her offspring, even in the face of great consequences. To flaunt and showcase his superiority to a mere woman, Ezemuo, the chief priest of Idemili shrine, labels Agbomma as the chosen priestess of Agbala oha shrine to be confined in a forest. A crucial point of suspicion to Ezemuo's action is the fact that he brought the message himself, a message which ordinarily is to be announced by the current priestess of Agbala Oha if it were to be true. Agwudo and his household find

213

this strange, but being conservative, he believes Ezemuo's office should not be challenged and therefore resigns himself to fate. Egoyinbo is having none of these, knowing fully well, it is a conscious attempt by Ezemuo to punish her using his office. This is because of her refusal to accept Ezemuo's advances, after he mistakenly sees her nakedness at river.

The docile Egoyibo at the beginning of the play, gradually becomes a Womanist who will not allow injustice on herself or her child. Egoyibo tries fervently; to make her husband understand that Ezemuo is being deceitful, but instead he shuts her up by asking "what do you know? I don't blame you; because I allowed you to talk does not mean I do not know what to do as a man!" (p. 32). One would expect that since Egoyibo knows that Ezemuo's claim is false, she should be able to challenge him directly or better still, table her case before the elders. This is a community strongly built on patriarchy; therefore, no one would listen to her case. This is confirmed in Egoyibo's response to her daughter Agbomma, Agbomma asks her to say no to the council of elders and Ezemuo. But the reality is:

> **EGOYIBO**: (*sighs*) I can say no, my daughter, but it will be like the sound of a loud fart, which escapes from in between faeces. No one listens to it, talk less of acting on it… never agree to be initiated as the priestess of Agbala oha. Reject it in your mind. If your father says there is nothing he can do; there is something we can do, you and me. (pp. 46-47).

This gives a perfect insight on the fate of the women in Umueze community. If a woman tries to voice her problem, no one listens because she is an ordinary woman or worse a 'drama queen', as such women are often labelled. Moreso, Ezemuo steps up his chauvinistic game upon suspicion that Agwudo may change his mind about releasing his daughter. His statement derogates the pride of womanhood:

> **EZEMUO**: The mouth of women is not as sweet as what lies in between their legs. It must be checked! Women are fickle minded; they cannot comprehend the mystery of our tradition, and that is why man is their head. Remember it is only the men that gather when the giant *Ikolo* drums or the sacred ekwe calls (p. 34).

From the above, it can be understood that men see women as second-class citizens in the society. In fact, the woman is only seen through her sexuality, and portrayed as one with low Intelligence Quotient. Egoyibo's protest gives us a lucid understanding of what she has been through as a woman who has experienced multiple child death. She is made to look like she is the maker of her life, and as such, she is responsible for the entire fault in her existence. For example, Ezemuo feels Egoyibo is the cause of her own trouble; he says "woman, hold yourself, it is not my fault that your stomach is full of *ogbanje*" (p. 36), thereby suggesting it is all her fault. This makes her resolved to fight Ezemuo to protect her only child. As the Womanist, she is not only fighting for herself, but for the survival of the entire community. This is because installing a wrong priestess means doom for her society. Through her strength, resistance and ploy, she can protect Agbomma from being confined to a forest where she only lives on people's sacrifices whenever they deem fit to offer, she is also able to avert the impending loom on her community. Eventually, Egoyibo embraces sisterhood and is able to protect everyone through the support of her fellow woman

215

Chika; who was hitherto seen as a non-conformist to culture and an over liberated woman without formal education. Ezemuo encounters death as the reward of his sin; wanting to play god.

Dramatization of the Female Energy in *Adaugo*

The play *Adaugo* by Osita Ezenwanebe documents the life of the female eponymous character Adaugo whose husband is going through a very rough time. Chuma, Adaugo's husband is an egoistic man who believes that no matter the problem a man is facing, he is not supposed to seek for help, as it will be termed begging. Chuma's ridiculous conclusion makes him prey to insecurity and irrational assumptions about his wife. Ezenwanebe uses the metaphor "daughter of an eagle" to describe Adaugo. In her words, "the eagle is considered a good symbol for the conception of womanhood and the end of the womanist method in *Adaugo*... the eagle of womanhood in this study resides in the remarkable strength of the female protagonist *Adaugo*" (Ezenwanebe 2012: 100). Likening Adaugo to an Eagle allows the reader picture her strength.

The play starts on the premise of encouragement and support. Adaugo encourages her husband to rise again after his epic business fail, but all her efforts prove abortive as Chuma is not willing to yield. Adaugo takes care of herself and family with her meagre salary; instead of praises and support, all she gets from her husband are meaningless accusations and insults. Even though Ezenwanebe tries to portray Chuma as being arrogant only because he is broke, from the subtext we can deduce that although being broke is part of Chuma's problem, the feeling of superiority is his main problem. Chuma's attitude can be viewed from Ezenwanebe's (2012: 98) submission where she says that "in Igbo patriarchal culture, the father or the eldest male is the head of the family and lineage is traced along the male line. Men therefore, occupy certain positions of power from which women are largely excluded".

One tends to conclude that the only reason Chuma and Adaugo's marriage seems to have survived in the past is because he had money to control and intimidate his wife. Clearly, he feels Adaugo has rendered no help to the family but only brag of her 'wealth' (meagre salary). He interprets every action of his wife as being controlling, and being proud, it makes him act like a time bomb waiting to explode. It cannot be concluded that all men are like Chuma because Uche's character is different and more understanding. However, the myth that 'many African men would not want their wives' achievements to be above theirs' may be true to some extent. This should not be viewed as male bashing, but as an expression precipitated by Chuma's action and that of some African men who see successful women's action as power tussle.

Chuma, like other oppressive patriarchal men, makes sure everything his wife says becomes an argument, which he turns around to make her feel like a bad woman; whereas he is the insecure one. Many women of today face similar challenges in their homes but choose to contain it within themselves in fear of the society labelling them as arrogant and insurbodinate. This feeling of entitlement and right to use power is the same one that drives Chuma about. Ultimately, he feels he must stay in control always; therefore, his wife handling monetary affairs at home means to him that he is beneath her. As a Womanist, Adaugo believes in complementing her husband, and as such sees the family's problem as 'our' problem, not his problem. Whereas Chuma uses words like "this is my house, and I have the right to

217

do whatever I feel like" (p. 26) to remind her she is nothing but a subordinate. Although Chuma switches to a loving husband occasionally, he snaps back quickly, as soon as his insecurity sets in.

> **CHUMA**: *Ugom, you are really* my crown, you are still the Adaugo I married. Thanks for the food I was already dying of hunger. What I ate in the afternoon was very small.
> **ADAUGO**: You need to eat well now to avoid adding ulcer to the list of our misfortune.
> **CHUMA**: I know *o*. But where is the money to feed well?
> **ADAUGO**: I will continue to try my best. Thank God I resisted the temptation to stop working. What would have become of us now? (p. 32).

Adaugo's courage, perseverance and her resolution to stand up for herself and children portray her as a dauntless woman. She stands up to her husband; when she calls for help, Chuma insinuates the action to mean begging. Adaugo responds thus:

> **ADAUGO**: I am not turning you into a beggar; it is the circumstance! Nor does being a woman means being a beggar. If I had gone for the training I agitated for, I would have been earning much more now. But no! You wouldn't let me. Now, look at how ugly everything has turned out. (p. 34).

Adaugo endures all sorts of assault from her husband and is 'submissive' enough to the point of burying her career for Chuma's wish. He would not let her train herself further and has attempted to stop her from working, but for her resilience. She uses overtly persuasive tone to avoid unnecessary arguments, yet

Chuma does not give up hauling abusive words at her. Another instance of confrontation is when he challenges Adaugo's effort to secure their children's school fees. She says to him "well, you said I was begging. Do I need your permission to beg? Chuma please it has been a very stressful day for me. Now I need rest, if you don't mind. *(Tries to leave; CHUMA draws her back.)*" (p. 48). He accuses her of sleeping around and calls her offensive and demeaning names. This he does to make her feel inferior and subsequently lower her self-esteem:

> **ADAUGO**: Chuma, you are looking for trouble. Who says you are in a better position to tell me who is to borrow money from? I know myself, I know what I want. I can take reasonable decisions. As a wife can't I make choices?
>
> **CHUMA**: That's not going to work in this house. I am your husband: the head of this family.
>
> **ADAUGO**: I am your wife; I'm the neck, not the tail of this family.
>
> **CHUMA**: I don't care what you are, neck or tail or both; but as long as you remain under my roof, you are under my authority (pp. 49-50).

The metaphor of Adaugo being the 'neck' of the family implies that she is the main support system. It also correlates with the Womanist theory, which believes in the partnership of both genders. The neck in the body holds and supports the head from falling. Therefore, whatever Chuma thinks of himself, it is only with Adaugo's support that he is an achiever. Uche's admonition to Chuma further corroborates this metaphor. He says:

> **UCHE**: You can rely on your wife for the time being, yes. She is there to support and complement you... which traditional culture

banned from contributing financially to the upkeep of the family? But you, Eddy, never stop praising your mother who ensured that hunger did not kill you and your siblings in school because your father would pay only the school fees while your mother provided for all other things. Chuma, the earlier you keep your pride in check and face reality, the better for you (p. 54-55).

Despite Chuma's egoistic tantrums, Adaugo is able to ensure the kids get back to school without delay. As Chuma irritabilities rises, he resorts to domestic violence to assert his hegemonic posture over Adaugo. Although, Ezenwanebe does not resolve the crisis of failed business which is the supposed genesis of Chuma's irritation, Adaugo tactically prove her innocence on the accusation of adultery with Uche for money. It turns out, Eddy, the crafty chauvinist, whom Chuma chooses as a friend is the one making passes at her at the same time ridiculing her husband. Unfortunately, Adaugo's situation is the sad reality for many Nigerian women, who are not as privileged as Adaugo. It is only when women decide to awaken their inner strength and resist subservience, that they will be able to rise against domineering cultures of the patriarchal society.

Conclusion

Osita Ezenwanebe's *Shadows on Arrival* and *Adaugo* are attempts to explore the plight of women in both modern and rural society, and how they have been able to manoeuvre their ways out of oppression using their Feminine power. The patriarchal society will always try to subjugate women, but using their strength and energies, women's resilience will become meaningful. From these plays, it is observed that women can rise against subservience without violence, and only they can shape their lives significantly and truthfully. This is to agree with a Yoruba proverb loosely translated as "the child who stretches her hand is the one the mother lifts up". Therefore, before the society joins the feminist struggle, the women must tactically cry out, enjoy public sympathy and subtly challenge the patriarchal institutions. Only then can they make progress with their struggle for equity.

It is apparent that Ezenwanebe, in her plays explores the tenet of Womanism that supports family ideals. A family makes up a society; therefore, whatever happens within families, directly or indirectly affects the society. When a woman lacks a voice in her home, she automatically will not be able to stand up against all other forms of oppression outside the home. Which is why stressing the fact that a woman is there to complement a man and not to be trampled upon is important.

It is recommended that women should believe in themselves and try to form bonds to help each other grow. Also, female writers should continue to advocate for female empowerment, as no matter how subtle or fierce the message is passed, it has an impact on the female folk. It allows them to discover to and rediscover ways of exploring their energies towards the achievement of fair treatment in the society.

REFERENCES

Azuike, M. (2011). "The female psyche in Irene Salami's *The queen sisters"*, in: Salami-Agunloye, I. (ed.), *African Women drama and performance*. Boston: Evergreen Books, pp.46-50.

Alao, A. & Ogundeji, T. (2014). "Women empowerment in the film industry", in Ogundeji, T. (ed.), *Dimensions of the new Nigerian Theatre: Critical essays in honour of Kola Oyewo*. United Kingdom: Alpha Crownes Publishers, pp. 156-168.

Ebo, E.E. (2009). "Women empowerment and the ideology of revolt in Irene Salami-Agunloye's *More than dancing and Sweet revenge*", in: Idegu, E. U (ed.), *Feminist aesthetics and dramaturgy of Irene Salami- Agunloye*. Kaduna: TW Press and Publishers, pp. 392-419.

Ezenwanebe, O. (2010). *Adaugo*. Ibadan: Kraft Books Limited.

Ezenwanebe, O. (2012). "The eagle of Womanhood", *Ofo: Journal of Transatlantic Studies*. 2(2): 97-113.

Ezenwanebe, O. (2013). *Shadows on arrival*. Ibadan: Kraft Books Limited.

Idegu, E.U. (2009). "Historical overview, global outlook, topical relevance and applicability of feminism", in Idegu E. U (ed.), *Feminist aesthetics and dramaturgy of Irene Salami- Agunloye*. Kaduna: TW Press and Publishers, pp. 73-87.

Ojediran, O. (2014). "Womanist view and political stance in Bakare Ojo Rasaki's selected plays", in: Adeoye, A.A., Nwaozuzu, U., Ejeke, S. & Akwang, E. (eds.), *Uncommon artistry: Understanding Bakare, Ojo Rasaki's dance, drama and theatre*. London: SPM Publications, pp. 162-175.

Salami-Agunloye, I. (2011). "Female power and the market women in Nigerian drama", in Salami-Agunloye, I. (ed.), *African women drama and performance*. Boston: Evergreen Books, pp. 86-103.

Sherry, R. (1989). *Studying women's writing: An introduction*. London: Edward Arnold Publishing.

THE FEMINIST AESTHETICS IN ZAYNAB ALKALI'S *THE STILLBORN*

Adenike ARINOMO

Introduction

Ism most times can be misunderstood as it is mostly considered a suffix that gives a better explanation of the adjunct word. Rather, ism is an ideology, a system of thought that carries along its own facts and theories. Feminism is located in Ism as a combination of two words; Femin and Ism. Feminism is not just fighting for women's right; it revolves around the experiences of women in relation to different perspectives. This means that Feminism is a developmental project of women by women for women irrespective of the means it takes to execute its function. These means are political, social, religious, cultural, and economic. Gubar (1985: 293) posits that:

> What led to feminist writing and criticism was culture. Our culture is steeped in such myths as male primacy in theological, artistic and scientific and creative endeavors. Feminist theologians who have shown that power is based on God the Father, and early writers who use terms or male titles such as Priest, Prophets, Legislator, Emperor to describe the man but the woman is described as being lower to the man

She further explains that some roles are not regarded as a woman's role in the society because the roles are considered more tasking and needs different skillsets to accomplish them, particularly skills that belong to *independent* individuals. Women are however regarded as *dependent*, and dependent on men, which is why the woman needs to be lower that the man. Gubar points out that this indirect discrimination led to the emergence of feminism. However, the need for women thinking for themselves arouse, and women started fighting for roles in the society. Hein (1990: 281) examines that "feminism creates new ways of thinking, new meanings and new categories of critical reflection". She further notes in the same place that:

> "feminism" does not pertain to women as the objects of love or hatred, or even of social (in)- justice, but fixes upon the perspective that women bring to experience as subjects, a perspective whose existence has heretofore been ignored.

What Hein has tried to explain here is that feminism is not defined by the love or hatred of women, rather it is defined by the experiences of women.

In the African tradition, the life of a woman is dominated by the sequential experience of birth, childhood, marriage, and finally womanhood. The exemption of a stage out of these stages is determined as a life that is futile. This chapter examines the ideologies of the perception of African women and the need to create feminist aesthetics. The further observation of this work does not only rely on feminism for women's right, but also to change the societal view of the capability of women which provides women with the opportunities to explore their latent abilities for social change.

The African Woman and African Female Novelist

The African female writers write from personal experience, the reality of their immediate environment, and society issues. The African female novelist writes on traditional and contemporary issues that involve the life style and experiences of African

224

women. The ideology of feminism is that Africa is different from the West as examined by Akung (2013: 27) that:

> Feminism in Nigeria is of a different mode and perspective compared to the Western brands of feminism. The differences in ideological perspectives have accounted for the many strands of feminism in Nigeria. These strands include womanism, motherism, stiwanism, femalism. But the dominant one has been womanism. Despite the different strands, one thing binds them together: the achievement of the common goal of liberating the Nigerian woman. Womanism became the dominant strand of African feminism when suddenly most Nigerian feminists came to terms with the fact that the radical and militant nature of Western feminism was out of place in Africa.

The African feminists have rejected those aspects of Western feminism that tend not to agree with African values because, even with feminism, the African culture cannot be totally ignored as it is a part and parcel of African women. Ogini (1996: 14) recognizes "that the needs of the black woman are not the same as those of the white woman, while equally affirming that the African woman has passed through a chain of oppressions under the system of patriarchy". One thing is clear here: the needs of the Western woman differ from those of the African woman.

As Ogini (1996: 14) puts it, "womanism desires that the man and the woman should be in harmony in the home and in the society at large". Ogini further explains that this contrasts the Western idea, where feminist writers and critics argue that the woman does not need the man. Marriages in the West could be contracted, and children may not be a part of it. Some call for lesbianism; for instance, Barbara Smith calls for women to learn getting sexual satisfaction outside the man. One must acknowledge the declaration of Ogini that "the womanist believes that the man and the woman have complementary roles of relationship". But the African tradition abhors a man or woman being alone, and children are seen as fruits of marriages. Infertility in either spouse is seen as society's tragedy. Ogini (1996: 18) states that:

> Womanism is a movement that celebrates the woman's strength as a pillar, the strength that brings black men to recognize and compromise for harmonious co-existence of both sexes. Womanism is a special culture that reminds men with special indication that without woman's full involvement in the system with the man is incomplete in action as well as in achievements.

This is present in the novels of Zaynab Alkali. In the *Stillborn*, irrespective of how bad Li's husband treats her, we are made to understand that this treatment is a result of the condition he finds himself which gives room for Li to reconsider going back to her husband as she needs him as much as he needs her.

The emergence of African feminist novel came as a reaction to the negative writings about the African women. The image of the African woman was being tampered with in the male writings and even in some female writings, and when the African feminist novelist discovered this, there was a sudden need to rise and protect the dignity of the African woman before it is totally shattered.

Feminism Aesthetics

Feminist theory is an integral part of women's studies and gender studies in the humanities. The forerunners of the feminist movement recognized earlier on the role of the Mass Media. Orjinta (2013: 77) mentions that:

> All these pioneers of feminism were writers: Mary Wollstonecraft wrote *A Vindication of the Rights of Women* (1792), Virginia Woolf, *A Room of One's Own* (1929, *A Room of One Alone*). Simone de Beauvoir published *Le deuxième Sexe* (*The Second Sex)* in 1949. While Wollstonecraft fought to improve the situation of women and their rights, Beauvoir was trying to encourage women to throw all sexist and stereotypical attitudes over board. Woolf wrote about conditions under which women could publish real literature (*écriture feminine*).

These pundits have therefore adopted literature as a virile medium of creating mass awareness and ignite the consciousness in the people. This exceptional campaign of self-discovery, empowerment determination to challenge the status quo, informs the notion of feminist aesthetics.

Aesthetics is known as uncommon, distinct, and a special kind of beauty that exists. It is the doing of something from the normal way into an exceptional way. Aesthetics is a means of capturing the viewer's breath by producing an extra-ordinary result. Hein (1990: 283) says "an aesthetic refers to a distinctive style of production". Distinctive in the sense that it differs from the usual method. The system of bringing out extra-ordinary out of the ordinary is known as aesthetics. Pushing beyond one's limit. Feminism aesthetics are the extra-ordinary characters, powers, and ideas that a woman possesses which are beyond the normal expectation. Feminism aesthetics sees the woman from a different perspective, relate with it, and brings out the very best out of it.

The first feminist aesthetics examines women's true nature; women's strength, weakness, courage, dreams, ideologies, desire and the ability to break beyond tradition in other to discover the hidden attributes and qualities of women in the society. The selected novel analyses the artistic impact and beauty of being a woman, the aspirations and trials of womanhood, the motherhood experiences, cultural limitations generated by some set of obnoxious traditions and the undaunted determination to change the social perception about women in the society.

The presentation of women in novels written by African male novelists has resulted in certain reactions by African female novelists. One of these African female novelists is Zaynab Alkali who has tried to bring another perspective of the female gender other than the usual representation of the African woman which portrays African women as the perpetrators of evil and bad events in the society. hooks (1984: 25) suggests that:

> When feminism is defined in such a way that it calls attention to the diversity of women's social and political reality, it centralizes the experiences of all women, especially the women whose social conditions have been least written about, studied or changed by political movements.

African feminists are found always struggling against the oppressive patriarchal tradition which subjugates, exploits, oppresses, and reduces them to inconsequential beings in the society. The women are not fighting with the opposite gender (male) *per se* but against societal norms and laws which have made them someone's appendage, thereby depriving them of their existence as legitimate individuals in their own society.

The true spirit of African feminism entails an abnegation of male protection and a determination to be resourceful and reliant. It follows therefore that for a woman to be free in the African patriarchal society; she must disregard restrictive traditional mores, struggle for self-assertion, demand her rightful place in the social set up of her society and have a spirit of independence as well as self-will to survive. This feminism spirit is demonstrated in the character of Li. Li disregards tradition by not waiting for her husband to call her back, rather, she decides not to go back to him in the city and chooses to further her education. She fights rigorously for her life and makes something out of it by managing to own her personal house and conquer the fear and trap of matrimony.

A reconstruction of Zaynab Alkali's novel unravels the ethical question of feminism through the use of feminist aesthetics to abrogate the ideology of women being the weaker vessel and being belittled, which leads to the need to stand firm in other to strengthen the female race. Alkali sees a woman as a being who can achieve any length with determination, through the portrayal of Li picking up her broken pieces when she wakes up from a dream and decides to go back to her husband even, in spite of what he had done to her. Therefore, feminist aesthetics is to help women to reason that the ideology of womanhood is beyond motherhood as there is the need to aspire for more out of life.

The major goal of African feminists is to ensure fair play, proper representation and due recognition of the woman both in the society and in literary works. They are not in any way fighting for equality with their male counterparts or attempting to overthrow the patriarchal authority. Ojediran (2013: 60) posits that "the female writers use their works to address and expose issues affecting women in their different continents in line with aesthetic differences and female identities". In relation to this, Alkali tries to fight for female identities using a specific part of Africa as her setting, mainly to portray that civilization has done a great deal to help the African women to rediscover themselves. For example, in Alkali's *The Stillborn*, Li's character is the opposite of Faku's. Li believes in female independence, while Faku believes in female being dependent on male. However, each reconciles with each other by learning that, either independent or dependent, their society did not give much room for their gender civilization growth and therefore they both fight for female gender growth and survival in the civilized era. To support this Irigarays (1995: 86) observes in an interview which Couze Venn interpreted in Women's Exile, and cited in Ojediran (2013: 60) that:

> The first step in the movements of women liberation is to enable every woman to become conscious that what she has felt in her own experience is a condition felt by all women which makes it possible for that experience to become politicized. Politicizing women's experience is not the type of politics instituted by men, but the politics that involves women's issue with regards to their contrasting tales.

This explains that the misdelineation, misunderstanding and misinterpretation of women is a global perception.

Feminist Aesthetics in Zaynab Alkali *TheStillborn*

The father of Zaynab Alkali came from Darin, a village in Borno State, Nigeria, but he moved to Gongola State where Zaynab was born and brought up in the early 1950s. She graduated from

Ahmadu Bello University with Bachelor of Arts degree in English before taking up the post of Principal (Head Teacher) of Shekara Girls' Boarding School, Kano from 1974 to 1976. In 1976, she was appointed a lecturer at Bayero University, Kano. She currently lectures in English and African Literature in English at the University of Maiduguri. She lives in Maiduguri with her husband and six children. Alkali is one of the first women novelists to emerge from Northern Nigeria; *The Stillborn* marks her debut. The novel reflects the author's belief that it is essential for women throughout Africa to be allowed and encouraged to fulfil their potential, if they are to make an effective contribution to the nations building. (Alkali, 1984: i).

Zaynab Alkali's *The Stillborn* is a novel set in a small village in the northern part of Nigeria around 1960. Nigeria had already obtained independence from Britain. The novel starts with a lorry carrying passengers on a journey to a small village. Despite the recklessness of the driver, the lorry arrives safely at the village and all passengers including the protagonist Li, alight. Li, whose real name is Mwapu, is the third of five children by Baba Garu; she is just arriving from the primary boarding school for holiday. Li is an intelligent girl who longs so much to leave the village for the city and start a city life. Together with her closest friend Faku and her elder sister Awa, Li and Faku dream of a better life in the city with a rich black man with plenty slaves. Awa meanwhile dreams of a better life in the village by getting married to the school headmaster. Nonetheless, life does not turn out the way they wish. Li ends up getting married to Habu who is also from her village, and together they live in a rented one-room apartment in the city. Habu begins a new lifestyle by coming home late and having other liaisons outside his marriage. Soon, a woman becomes pregnant for him. After a botched aborting during which the woman loses her womb, Habu is given the

231

option of marrying the woman or going to jail. He accepts to marry the woman. However, he cannot reveal the truth to Li, his wife. Not long after, Li goes home to attend her ill father. Faku meanwhile has married Garba from their village. She follows him to Kano where she discovers that he already has a wife and she (Faku) is now the second wife. Awa eventually marries the headmaster but soon the headmaster losses his job and becomes a drunkard. Nonetheless, Awa gives birth every year, raising the number of mouths to feed in an increasingly poor household.

Occupied with what life throws at them, the three women pick up their pieces and fight to make life a better place for them to live. Li, after leaving her husband for her father's burial and waiting endlessly for Habu to ask for her return, according to the tradition, decides to continue with her education. While in school, Habu visits her and invites her to come home. He confesses the problem he had with the lady he was forced to marry and pleads for Li to return home. He demands to see his daughter's picture, but Li refuses all his demands and dismisses him. She goes back to the village a fulfilled woman and even manages to own her personal modern building but, in the end, she returns to her husband's house.

Faku, on the other hand, is being treated as a second wife without any financial support from her husband. She leaves Garba's house to start a new life. Eventually she succeeds and becomes a successful business woman. Awa, the weakest of the girls, becomes the toughest as she is forced to have the responsibilities of heading Garu's family and to take care of her five children. She realises life is cruel and needs to be dealt with in tough ways.

Importantly in this novel, the first feminist aesthetics is that of awareness, which is the need to be more knowledgeable about something and the desire to know more through experience. The novelist realises this by making us understand that the female gender is quite inquisitive. Alkali ensures that her heroine, Li, rejects what for her is the claustrophobia of life in the village when, at the age of thirteen, she longs to leave her father's compound. When Li and her siblings discuss, and her brother Sule says that "No, God knows life should be better than this", Li retorts with, "As for me, big brother, I can't wait to get out of this hell" (p. 4).

The reason for these statements is because Li and her elder brother Sule both attend the primary boarding school outside their village. They have been exposed to a better life outside the village and Li wants freedom from both the village and her father. Under normal circumstance, being a girl restricts her aspiration in the community to that of a mother, but due to her exposure and education level, she has come to realise that there is more to life than being a wife. She now regards the home she once considered her safe haven a hellish place to be. Li's restlessness is only relieved when she manages to sneak out of the house to meet Habu Adams who eventually becomes her husband. Li's grand-father Kaka does not see much future in tradition which blinds the eyes of Li's father. He warns that "children shouldn't be caged... for if the cage got broken by accident or design, they would find the world too big to live in" (p. 25). It is essentially in this sense of social incarceration that Li rejects her home which she now perceived as "hell".

Another feminist aesthetics is submission and rebellion. Alkali describes these two words as words that work alongside of each other. She brings out the beauty of duality of life which says, "for every good thing there must be a bad side and for every bad side there must be a good side". Alkali makes us to understand that the female gender can be submissive as well as rebellious; submissive in the terms of fear and trying to keep peace and rebellious in the term of trying to discover more. Alkali makes use of Li and her sister Awa to explore this aesthetics. "I see", Awa laughed. "Well I really want to watch the dance to the newly composed song. Have heard the dance steps are complicated, but you know how impossible it is to get out of this place" (p. 14).

With Awa's view, it is obvious that she really wants to attend the dance, but something is stopping her from doing so. This next sentence makes us understand why she cannot attend the dance. "You devil", Awa sounded worried. "I will come with you but we won't stay long and you must behave yourself. Someone close to father might see us. You know very well what he thinks of Cultural dances" (p. 15). It is clear from this exchange that Awa is scared of her father's reaction if she were to attend the dance. The only way to keep the peace in the house is for her to obey his rules. Alkali is emphasising here that the fear of the male gender by the female is the reason for submissiveness to the rules by Awa. However, Alkali provides a solution to the undue submissiveness by creating rebellious aesthetics in the characters. "He won't learnt of this", Awa replied. "And if he does, we will have to pay for it" (p. 16). There is a hint here that with the flouting of the male rule comes repercussions, but the punishment would be worth the while as long as the original offence serves to crack the patriarchal system.

Alkali's portrayal of rebellious aesthetics shows that the female gender can only be rebellious once there is an exposure beyond her comfort zone. Li is however audacious because of her education; she is aware that if she breaks the rule, the punishment would only seek to reinforce the rule. One of the ways in which Alkali explores the reason for rebellious acts of women is thus by placing Li in confrontational situations with her father. Her first confrontation is when her father demands that she stop singing filthy songs. "Good. I am tired of filthy songs in my compound; he said, and Li let out a sigh. Baba heard and shouted at her. Li turned and stared at him fearlessly" (p. 9). Without fear, Li asserts her sense of independence. Considering the extract, which illustrates Li's *unnatural* and sudden lack of submission and even her outright aggression, gives room for continuous rebellion shortly after the incident of the songs. Li sneaks out of the compound at night without her father's permission but instead of confessing or being contrite, she displays a kind of aggression that demonstrates that she is beginning to enjoy the game with her father. "Li no longer looked fidgety. Her eyes grew bold. She was beginning to enjoy the drama" (p. 23). The battle line is drawn and the conflict agenda is set between submitting to the patriarchal rules or asserting an awareness that privileges femininity and engagement. Li now realises that her reactions have powerful consequences, as her father inevitably concedes 'defeat' over the 'little' matters of harmless disobedience.

Alkali has made us understand that once a female gender can fight back and claim a proper right, then a détente or compromise situation can be achieved. The novel suggests that Baba recognizes but equally fears his daughter's *fearlessness*: "Li had the power to stir such emotions in him. He thought she was impudent, but it wasn't just this that worried him. It was something else" (p. 9). Here, Baba seems to be disarmed by Li's ability to outwit him in confrontation: "If Baba insisted on beating Sule, she was going to confuse the whole issue by confessing. That way Baba would never know who actually went out, and he wasn't one to punish anyone if in doubt. Li smiled wickedly. It seemed to her that that was one of Baba's few virtues" (24).

Another aesthetic examined in the novel is that of determination. "Don't worry about me, Li. I am alright. Go to the village, and when you get there, say this for me to my mother. The land is still brown and unyielding, not until it is covered with grain will I come to the village" (p. 18). Faku, in making this statement, expresses Alkali's understanding of the importance of language, lore, and proverbs. The statement means that Faku is determined not to go back to the village until she has become successful and prosperous. This is determination portrayed by a woman who is yet to achieve any of her plans. Alkali posits here that even though the female is considered the weak vessel, determination makes her far stronger. With all the disappointment Faku has faced in the city, including getting married as the second wife without any financial support from her husband, she is determined not to go back to the village but as a conqueror.

Feminism fights for the assertiveness of the female gender, yet, ironically, the woman belittles herself. Alkali portray this in Li. Li intends to be the most educated woman in the village and for miles around. Only then will she assume the role of the "man of the house" in her father's compound (p.85). Becoming a "man of the house" does not connote that she seeks equality with the male power. Simply, it means she wants to be independent and be in a position to live her life the way she wants and to make rules for herself. Nonetheless, Li belittles herself, thinking the only reason she could attain the role of a "man of the house" would be through schooling. At the end of the novel, Li goes back to her husband and her sister Awa who is not as educated as Li and becomes the man of the house by providing the decision-making leadership role that is needed. Alkali is trying to clarify that

236

education is not the only criterion for female gender to measure up to male gender; it is the ability and resilience of any of the sexes that makes up the individual.

One other feminist aesthetics is the need to be dependent. In as much as the woman claims to be capable of all things there is a part of her which hopes for a shoulder to put her body upon.

> It is not true, Sule. Faku also had a dream, a deep need for security. She had grown up without a father, she yearned for a man's presence in her home. I remember her saying and I can still see the glow on her face as she said it 'a man's moody shoes outside my door! A man's commanding voice in the early hours of the day and late hours of the night. Where indeed is the lord of the house who brings in food for his obedience wife to cook?' No, Sule, if any of us didn't mean to drift it was Faku, but Gaba could not understand he failed to fill that vacuum in her life (p. 99)

Earlier before this statement, Sule accuses Faku of being being a prostitute, which he believes is the reason Gaba left her. But the sentiments above gives us an understanding that irrespective of how strong the female, there is always the pressure to be dependent on a man. But the failure to be able to depend on this male makes woman stronger to fight her battles and provide solution for herself.

The Feminist aesthetics of marriage is also presented as a discourse by Zaynab Alkali. This is a fantasy that lies within the African mentality towards marriage; the issue of marrying off girls and teenagers at an early age. The Africa society did not encourage the idea of girl child education which is one reason for early marriage for most women. This is one of the strands in Alkali's novel. Even though Li is educated to some extent, she still hangs on the fantasy of marriage. For instance, she wants to attend the dance for the simple reason that if men think that a young teenage girl is ripe for marital responsibilities, the same girl should be allowed to exercise some form of independence. "Well, it is just that our mother was taken to her husband house at the age of fourteen" (p. 14). If Li's mother became married at fourteen, then Li should be trusted to go to a dance. But the main reference here is the revelation that women such as Li's mother were married off at a tender age.

Another ideology of marriage is the fact that if a marriage breaks up without a child, there is the possibility that the marriage is irreparably over. However, a child provides the hope of reconciliation to an estranged couple. Li, at the end of the novel, goes back to her husband, to the bafflement of her sister. "Awa shook her head thoughtfully. You are going back to him?" (p. 105). This is a rhetorical question. Awa is aware of her sister's change of heart. After all, Li has a child for Habu and the reason he maltreated her in the marriage was due to the circumstances around the period, even though he brought it on himself. Apart from the child between them, Alkali presents another feminine aesthetics – a soft-hearted woman. Even though she has been previously hurt, she still finds a reason to go back to her husband.

Alkali explores another feminist aesthetics surrounding the tradition of courtship. When a young man approaches a woman for courtship, the expectation is that the woman exercise restraint so that she does not give the impression that she is wayward or lacks discipline. The woman usually does this by repelling the approaches of the man, often by rude responses and retorts. In contrast, the man's seriously is measured by his composure while being insulted or rebuffed by the woman. This is clearly explicated in the novel. For instance, at the dance, the following awkward conversation takes place between Habu and Awa:

> "Why aren't you two dancing? He asked with a worried expression. Same reason you are not. Awa answered his question coldly" (p. 18)
> [...]
> "May we live to see tomorrow, girls? Greet your people for me he added. Uhmmmm', Awa grunted, see who is sending his greetings to my people "(p. 19)

Even though Awa and Li are both there, Awa is the first to snap at Habu continuously which Li regards rude.

The debate about the nature of the urban woman and the rural woman is complicated. The urban woman considers the rural one uneducated, submissive and sometimes downright ignorant, with no awareness of modern reality and civilized behaviour. On the hand hand, the rural woman considers her urban counterpart disrespectful and a bad example of what a woman should be in the society. This is another aesthetics that Alkali explores in the novel. Alkali posits that even though the urban woman has some advantage over the rural woman, which is exposure to modern living, there are yet some aspects of civilisation that do not clearly engage with the realities of an African society. Garba cites one example of this, by raising the differences between the cost of organizing a marriage in the city, which is more expensive than a similar venture in the village or rural areas. In contrast, Alkali highlights the morality of city living. "A girl could live with you of her own free will, sometimes you do not have to pay anything; Garba continued" (p. 45). This would not be acceptable or even probable in the village where the sense of propriety is more advanced and where the familiarity among the people would not allow such non-traditional union. Alkali reacted to this from the perspective of the African woman. In relation to Garba's statement above, "That is not marriage, Awa exploded with indignation. That's prostitution" (p. 46). Awa is here stressing the importance of feminine dignity in African society. Living with a man without the institution of marriage is undignified

With this, Koroye (1989: 47) perceives a significant shift in Alkali's writing compared to other African writers:

> Mrs. Alkali's subject is (perhaps, predictably) woman, but her treatment of it indicates a remarkably new emphasis which is different in degree, if not in kind, from the feminist positions made familiar by novelists like Flora Nwapa and Buchi Emecheta. An ascetic vision of the truly liberated woman informs the theme as well as the style of *The Stillborn*.... For the image of the new woman – not a stillbirth, but a fully formed, independent person that The Stillborn presents is inscribed all over with the ascetic ideals of 'determination' and 'virtue': roles and identity allotted a woman by a male-dominated society; and virtue in being able at the same time to forgive and redeem the man or men in her life.

With her last sentiments of the novel, Alkali sends a message to every woman, which explains the similar nature of both male and female in the society, and especially in the kind of relationships that lead to oneness and mutual understanding:

Awa shook her head thoughtfully. You are going back to him?

Yes!

Why, Li? The man is lame; said the sister

We are all lame, daughter of my mother. But this is no time to crawl. It is time to learn to walk again (p. 105).

The female experience defines the feminine aspirations in the society, and this can only be achieved with dedicated determination towards attaining and sustaining feminine virtues.

Conclusion

This chapter has explored and examined feminism in a sustained mode; the portrayal of African women in literature; the reason for the emergence of African female writers; and the examples of feminist aesthetics in an African literature. Alkali attempts to provide possible answers to some gender questions, using the actions of some female characters in *The Stillborn*. She explores the philosophy of beauty, arts and life experience to suggest changes to the social ideology of the female in the society. She posits issues of conflict and resolution towards tradition through the use of these aesthetics. Finally, she advocates viable options and solutions for African women who are in a dilemma or who are yet to rediscover their sense of femininity in an age of decreasing gender disparity.

REFERENCES

Akung, J. (2013). "The western voice and feminist criticism of the Nigerian novel", *World Journal of English Language*. 3(1); 24-37.

Alkali, Z. (1984). *The Stillborn*. Lagos: Longman.

Amase, E. T. A. and Kaan, A. (2014). "Is Zaynab Alkali merely a feminist writer? An appraisal

Of *The Stillborn* and *The virtuous woman*", *Ijalel: International Journal of Applied Linguistic and English Literature.* 3(3); 188-194.

Davies, C. B. (1986). "Introduction: Feminist consciousness and African literary criticism", in Davies, C. B. & Graves, A. A. (eds.), *Ngambika: Studies of women in African literature.* Trenton, N.J: Africa World Press, pp. 1-23

Frank, K. (1987). "Women without Men: The feminist novel in Africa", *African Literature Today.* Lagos: Nigeria.

Gordon, T. (1990). *Feminist Mothers.* London: Macmillan Education Ltd.

Gubar, S. (1985). "The blank page and the issue of female creativity", in Showwalter E. (ed.), *The new feminist criticism.* New York: Pantheon Books, pp. 292-313.

Hadjitheodorou, F. (1999). *The creative transformation of women in African literature.* Pretoria: University of Pretoria.

Hein, H. (1990). "The role of feminist aesthetics in feminist theory", *The Journal of Aesthetics and Arts Criticism* (Autumn), 48(4); 281-291.

Hooks, B. (1984). *Feminist theory from margin to center.* Boston: Southend Press.

Koroye, S. (1989). "The Ascetic feminist vision of Zaynab Alkali", in Otokunefor, H. & Nwodo, O. (eds), *Nigeria female writers: A critical perspective.* Lagos: Malthouse Press Limited.

Ogundipe-Leslie, M. (1987). "The female writer and her commitment", *Women in African Literature Today*. London: James Curry Ltd.

Oko, E. (1994). "Issues of gender images of women in Nigerian writings", *Ndunode: Calabar Journal of Humanities*, 1(1); 66-79.

Ojediran, O. (2013). "Womanist aesthetics of assertiveness in Zulu Sofola's *Wedlock of the gods, The Performer: Ilorin Journal of The Performing Arts*, 15(6); 56-67

Orjinta, A. (2013). *Womanism as a Method of Literary Text Interpretation: A Study of Emergent Women's Images under Religious Structures in Selected Works of Heinrich Böll*, Inaugural-Disseration zur Erlangung des Doktorgrades der Philosophie an der Ludwig-Maximilians-Universität München, Munchen. Nsukka, Nigeria: University of Nigeria Press Ltd.

THE STATUS AND IMAGE OF WOMEN IN SELECTED WORKS OF NIGERIAN WRITERS

Oludolapo OJEDIRAN

Literatures by and on women are still emerging, as the debates on their relevance have become more engaging. There have been increasing revelation of the transformation and changes to the social images and identity of women, as revealed in successive conferences devoted to women's issues. Starting from the First World Conference on Women in 1975 at Mexico City to the Second World Conference on Women at Copenhagen in 1980, the Third World Conference on Women in 1985, and the Beijing conference of 1995, the importance of literatures on women has become more emphasized.

The Beijing conference of 1995 titled Fourth World Conference on Women: Action for Equality, Development and Peace, created in the mind of women the agitational consciousness to gain the needed freedom and voice in any patriarchal society. Although there had been meetings, workshops and views from women who see male domination, female autonomy and ownership of their beings as something that needs to be revisited, the outcome has not been positive like that of 1995 where women became more aware of what needed to be done. While Beijing Conference deliberated on women's empowerment and equality between women and men, several literatures by female writers that came up after the conference started taking more assertive positions in order to reflect how a woman should live and be empowered within a phallic society.

While this work is not on the overview on women's conferences that have taken place or yet to be organized, such conferences are often seen as an avenue that created chances for women to be outspoken and a way of negotiating the public sphere which is the male domain. Ironically, such conferences are seen as platforms where values and women's conditions are recognised and where they discuss which invariably affects the writings of the female gender. Obafemi (1989: 42) advises Sofola that:

> It is high time Zulu Sofola used the position of influence and pre-eminence she enjoys as a leading female dramatist in Nigeria, to positive and pertinent ends. She must move away from old school and depict realities of today. Rather than advocate the continued subjugation of the female folk in particular and humanity in general... she should strive towards the emancipation of her sex, in particular, and the liberation of humanity in general, from enslaving codes icons and ideas.

As the first published Nigerian female playwright, Sofola enjoyed patronages from male and female readers, some out of curiosity and others out of joy. Her early plays *King Emene, Old Wine are Tasty,* and *Wedlock of the Gods* tend towards protecting cultural values laid down by men. However, after much discourse about writing to create females with stereotypic perspectives about womanhood, she wrote *The Ivory Tower* (unpublished). She created Kemetia, a female with zeal and passion who fight against cultism in the University. Getting her inspiration from African heroines such as Moremi of Ile-Ife, Queen Amina of Zazzau and Winnie Mandela of South Africa, Kemetia is depicted as a woman of action. Through this character, Sofola presents to the readers how a woman should be motivated to rise against female marginalisation and male egoistic domination. While some female writers write to create a gender-balanced society, others write to create the positive images for women by giving their female characters the social awareness of identity and self-assertion. Recently, Obafemi and Yerima (2004: 55) agree that Sofola's:

> Mastery in handling the strengths and weaknesses of her women is what makes her tragic plays socially realistic. Being a woman herself, Sofola writes from an intimate knowledge of her female characters. But from her many plays with dominating female characters, it is the traditional plays and the portrayal of the female characters that have been most successful. The reason for this is that Sofola's perception of what her plays advocate, regarding the cause of the modern woman, is often not agreeable with the modern feminist ideological persuasion.

This is explicit in Sofola's characters, Odibei and Obiageli in Wedlock of the Gods, whom she portrays as women who are traditional in their outlook. Creating tragic scenarios for both characters brings out their traditional maternal instinct within the patriarchal culture that cherishes male children. Ironically, while Sofola tries to see these women as active, vengeful and embittered, their anger is directed at other women and not the patriarchal system.

However, whilst women are being victimised all over the globe, the Third World women are more at the receiving end than those of the Western world. Women are victimised not only by the men but also by themselves, which is one of the thematic considerations of discourse in works by female writers. While this collection deals mainly with the Nigerian women, it also reveals that irrespective of ethnicity, background, race, colour, age, qualification, and status, amongst other matters, women issues are the same because they are in an enclosed patriarchal system; going through the same agonies and uncertainty and obeying the same laws. Though, so many things have changed in most societies especially in the Western world through Women's Rights movements, the Nigerian system is only just gradually following suit.

Within the creation of literary works, sexual, economic, emotional, cultural and social exploitations are seen in different dramatic forms. As this work views the female literary traditions as the medium through which women's victimisations and subjugations are exposed, such works also provide alternative positions to women's existence in the patriarchal system. Such alternatives are identified by Abacha (1997:20):

> Women, as wives, mothers and family members have a duty not only to protect the core values of society, but to ensure that they propagate such values through the process of socialization and information dissemination... In a world where information is power, access to control over and sharing of information and knowledge are crucial elements in women's participation and empowerment.

Abacha sees that women have specific roles to play in the attainment of self-empowerment by using the information they pass across from one generation to the other for themselves. Women should not only be cultural projectors, rather they should use such projected cultural values to protect and fight for themselves. For example, Ebikere's character in Julie Okoh's *Edewede* and Adesua in *Aisha* are presented as mothers who protect cultural values over femalehood. They see culture as something that supersedes any human being despite that culture is never static, that some cultural norms could be limiting and

247

retrogressive or passive and subservient with women at the receiving end. Okoh presents binary characters who can go against such subservient cultural practices. Edewede in *Edewede* is seen as a woman of zeal, self-determination and uncompromising attitudes which leads to her repudiation, but at the end, she is able to fight for the needed freedom. Iriata summarises this in the play that:

> We are women. We love being women, wives and mothers. But each woman wants to be herself, think for herself and express herself in her own way as a unique being. Circumcision takes these rights from us, makes us objects. Today, we reject that status. We no longer live simply following the ideas handed over to us. So, ban circumcision, real Edewede's repudiation or forget about us (p. 44).

Affirmative / Independent Woman

Affirmative and independent female characters show that Nigerian women are ready and prepared to change their positions from the docile, inaudible and voiceless to the affirmative and socially independent woman who can be in spaces of authority. Such women take their place of power and can be seen as a woman of substance filled with integrity, dignity and personality. Rather than being socio-culturally or religiously suppressed, the women are ready to boldly showcase and celebrate their gender. This category of women is presented as individuals or people who, despite the limitations of the patriarchal culture, refuse to be suppressed, dominated and muted. Nwapa (2007: 527) gives an answer to how African writers project women in their works. She sees that "a few of them have tried to project an objective image of women, an image that reflects the reality of women's role in the society". Yet some writers still create women who are

248

caricatures of human existence. For example, in Chinua Achebe's *Things Fall Apart*, Okonkwo's part as the traditional head of the family portrays the typical Nigerian patriarchal system whereby a man's decision goes unchallenged. Achebe presents the egoistic and boastful nature of man where physical and psychological abuse of a woman is seen as a normal phenomenon. Although, creative writings have moved beyond this, Achebe's creative imagination is seen by Acholonu (1994: 40) as an act of women brutalisation that is due to illiteracy, rusticism and morbid traditionalism. The rejection of these female stereotypes is presented in the works of Mabel Segun, Zainab Alkali, Zulu Sofola, Tess Onwueme, Julie Okoh, Irene Salami-Agunloye, Sefi Atta, Tracie Utoh-Ezeajugh, Osita Ezenwanebe, Stella Dia Oyedepo and others. These women writers write in order to pave ways for the alternative creation of women status whereby they can make immense positive contributions on issues such as marriage, childbirth, motherhood, and emotional psyches. Solberg (1983: 247) observes that one of the ways of correcting one's faulty image of the African woman would be through the African women seen from the ''inside'', in other words, rendered by women. Also, Showalter (1986: 14) sees that female writing has its own unique character whether because it draws on female body images, uses a 'woman' language, expresses the female psyche or reflects women's cultural position. Solberg and Showalter's views are seen from the literary perspectives whereby female writers should endeavour to recreate their positions in the society through literary values. It is true that when a woman writer writes from a woman's perspective about women's issues, the flavour and aesthetics embedded in such work is different from writing outside the female body since she is writing from experiences, inner self and perspectives. The women in this category reject what Stubbs (1981: xiii) observes and embraces that:

a. No matter what part in society individual women in fact play, traditional images focus on their domestic and sexual roles. This has the effect continually limiting women's notion of themselves and their possibilities. It undermines from within... the women's movement knows this, and so attempts to combat cultural stereotypes of female experience...

b. These are confronted and hopefully discredited by the creation of new alternative images which instead of narrowing women's consciousness of themselves, try to expand it.

Stubbs' observation reflects the present situation among Nigerian female writers who are also products of same experiences. Most Nigerian female writers such as Zulu Sofola, Irene Salami-Agunloye, Julie Okoh, Tess Onwueme, and Osita Ezenwanebe are embracing the redefinition and re-appraisal of women in the society by creating females who act outside the domesticated and cultural roles expected of them. The writers create these roles in order to have alternative status like working class woman, strong willed, assertive and agile women while they destroy the old ones that see them as witches, harlots, fragile, and full house wife. These women are referred to by Afolabi (2002: 127) as "Womb-Men"; women who are ready to assert themselves and prove to men that they are capable of doing what they do. While women in this category take into cognisance that the physiognomic creations of both sexes are different by nature's design, they still see themselves as competitors in humanity. Such is the situation in Stella Oyedepo's *The Rebellion of the*

Bumpy Chested whereby the female characters in the play takes another dimension to fight for their freedom in a patriarchal society. Affirmative women are seen as models of self-determination, self-assertion and self-actualisation.

Oyedepo's female characters are what Ojediran (2012: 253) describes as women with aesthetics in assertiveness who view strong will as a form of help, the formation of a strong self which allows them to explore the opportunities of disagreeing with certain socio-cultural, historical and religious beliefs that limit and destroy their capabilities. However, writers who present female characters in this category see a woman as a whole being and not a fragmented part in their portrayal because they are either able to confront their situations or avoid the situations, as in Irene Salami-Agunloye's *More than Dancing* where women's consciousness and active participation are required to take their place in politics and social mainstream.

Also, in *The Queen's Sister,* Ubi's character is presented as a womanist stereotype who defies all instructions at the king's palace that her co-wives see her as the odd one amongst them. Women in this category help themselves to freedom as portrayed in Tracie Utoh-Ezeajugh's *Out of the Mask* where the women carry out their threats to the bewilderment of the men. Ifeoma is given the voice in the play to challenge the male characters who take advantage of the masquerades to molest women. In the engaging dialogue, it shows that women are becoming self-confident to see some archaic traditions as obsolete, worthy of abrogation by the society.

> **IFEOMA**: You won't do anything. If you think that this year is like other years that you molested us and went free, then try it and see. Go and tell the

251

other boys. If any masquerade flogs me tomorrow, I will set fire on that masquerade.

IZUNNA: Chai Abomination! Look at these female-things talking abomination about masquerade. The cabinet must hear this. It is taboo and you must suffer the punishment.

IFEOMA: Who cares about your useless taboo. You can't scare us. If you try any nonsense tomorrow, we will do something that will shock everybody who hears it.

OKEY: I am not surprised that you are making mouth. That is what women are good at (pp. 93-94).

Utoh-Ezeajugh uses the characterization of these four girls to challenge the culture that has marginalized and subordinated them for years. To the uttermost surprise of the boys and even to the readers, the playwright makes the girls wear mask which sends a message of confrontation to anyone. One cannot call this swapping of roles; rather it is seen as being assertive to make the necessary change needed within the patriarchal society. Just like we see in Julie Okoh's *Edewede* where the major character, Edewede, instigates her fellow women against the men, Utoh-Ezeajugh also brings out the character of Chisolum as a womanist character who is ready to fight the men to a standstill. This mirrors Alice Walker's view as a way of rescuing the marginalised woman from the negative and inaccurate stereotypes that masks her in the feminist discourse. Her definitions of womanism in the book *In Search of Our Mother's Garden's: Womanist Prose* (1983) sees that womanism is:

> The black folk expression of mothers to female children, you are acting womanish, i.e. like a woman… usually referring to outrageous, audacious,

252

courageous, or wilful behaviour. Wanting to know more and in greater depth than is considered 'good' for one... (A womanist is also) a woman who loves other women sexually and / or non sexually. Appreciates and prefers women's culture... and women's strength... committed to survival and wholeness of entire people, male and female. Not a separatist..." (pp. xi-xii).

Chisolum and Edewede express the womanish aesthetics whereby a young girl wants to know more than it is expected of her. The fearlessness and courage needed by women in general is seen in these two characters who does not see anything wrong in taking their fights to the people in question. While Chisolum agrees to be punished for the sins of the other girls, Edewede takes on the sex strike with other women of her age to stop the maltreatment from men. This shows that women are engaging themselves in their freedom if the society does not. This corroborates Salami's (2005: 423) view that:

Globally women have been known to use collective action to put pressure on the authorities in order to liberate themselves from on form of oppression or another. In Nigeria, examples of female collective actions against male intrusion into female spaces are known to have taken place.

Collective action is an act of sisterhood which allows women to be their sister's keeper. Such collective action is seen in Tess Onwueme's *The Reign of Wazobia*; Irene Salami-Agunloye's *Sweet Revenge*, and *Idia, the Warrior Queen of Benin*; and Tracie Utoh-Ezeajugh's *Our Wives Have Gone Mad Again*. Sisterhood helps women assert their identification with one another and claim a collective strength to fight against patriarchal culture. This view is embodied in the slogan that "sisterhood is powerful" , coined by Kathie Sarachid in 1968 and popularised in Robin Morgan's book *Sisterhood is Powerful* (1970). Although this phrase is common in the writings of so-called "radical feminists", the focus of their writing is arguably the rage of women against men. This is still common in women's writings who see their female characters as subsumed in externally imposed societal laws that negate both their personal and collective images.

Docile / Dependent Woman

This category of women refuses to see their worth as women, and care less about what they go through in the patriarchal system. They see the inferiorized and second-class position and the status quo in the society as what should continue particularly for women who have been in such system for a long time. The docile and dependent women dogmatically follow laid down tradition which they see as a way of life. Such women want stereotyped cultures of subjugation that continue to make them subordinates, dependent and passive. They are depicted in most literary works as good cooks, home cleaners, gossips, care givers. They are full of complexes that makes the woman socially irrelevant. The women are powerless as they are overwhelmed by domestic responsibilities and imposition of rules and responsibilities by men. They are usually discarded through a continuous social process that has limited them from girlhood. The character of Bharo in Julie Okoh's *The Mannequins* falls into this category of women who want to always be at the mercy of men, depend on them and be at the beck and call of men. Although they can be in the position of liberating themselves, they are not ready to change. Bharo, an uneducated fashionista is depicted as a woman with a mindset of accepting her stereotyped domestic role in the society. She is voiceless from the beginning of the play, accepts Mr. Adudu's sexual advances, believes in polygamy and respects the husband's rights irrespective of what she wants or deserves as a woman. This is a play where Okoh presents the men as people who acquire women as properties. Bharo's inability to tell her colleagues the source of her expensive travelling and extravagant lifestyle irritates Ekata who expresses his mind that:

> **EKATA**: I pity you. You are all body but no soul.
> Just like the mannequins in the supermarket. They
> look so attractive you think they are human
> beings. But have a close look at them, they are
> nothing but dead bodies (34).

Okoh's view of female voicelessness is summarised by Ekata who sees a woman with Bharo's attributes to be a decorated mannequin in the supermarket because she will forever remain silent and weighted down under an endless array of accessories.

Further, taking a clue from Irene Salami's *The Queen Sisters*, a play based on history, women are seen as mere acquisition of properties whereby a man's wealth is showcased and valued. Ubi, the heroine in the play is forcefully married to the King. Out of disgust, she rebels including against the co-wives. Salami-Agunloye presents this play in a new form required of women writers to change their stories in history and at present. Historically, Ubi is said to be a wicked woman who committed so many abominable acts and wicked deeds, but *The Queen Sisters* provides an alternative way of viewing women in history. This play showcases another form of stereotype through history that sees years of women's subordination and marginalisation. Azuike (2011: 47) asks vital questions that make the play a success such as:

255

...from what does Ubi plan to liberate the Benin women? Is it from the shackles of ignorance and superstition, which the women of the harem have, for years, willingly accepted? Could she be on a conscientization mission to challenge the "phallic dominance" of her society? How far will she succeed, indeed, to change the psyche of a society which has adhered strictly to a series of stereotypical views that have resulted in the general devaluation of women?

While Ubi's behaviour generated lots of controversies, anger and agitation as seen in Benin kingdom, the oppressive nature of the society is brought to lime light whereby women can read and be determined to change their stories from the docile and passive woman to the vocal and active person. Reading through the lines of Iyase and Osuma, one sees the position man expect woman to be up till now:

> **IYASE**: Our mothers were very well behaved. They submitted easily to our fathers. They never initiated any discussion and never joined in any unless they were asked to.
>
> **OSUMA**: They were hardly ever seen or heard in public affairs (p. 9)

Iyase and Osuma's comments are quite true in the past. This is visible in some traditional Nigerian societies where women are rarely admitted into the elder's councils except when she is to be reprimanded for any offence, or when she has become an elderly woman that they feel can keep secrets, a stage is referred to as "masculinity" in some cultures. To the men, this is a stage when she has evolved to the level where she can contribute useful ideas in the society. Disgracefully, issues that concerns women are also presided on(delete) over by men without considering how women feel or what they can do. Okoh (2003: 165) opines that:

> As society developed, gender discriminations are institutionalised and reinforced by traditions and religious dogma, until they become part of our cultural heritage; hence, in every patriarchal society, women are placed under the tutelage of men, first, of her father, then of her husband and is never viewed as an entity in her own capacity.

It is observed that culture plays an important role in the domestication of women and their perspective about life. Culture established the inequalities between the sexes. This gives the male gender greater and respected values in the world than the female ones. Taking a critical look at the cultural traditions that back a woman up in the Nigerian society, one sees that such traditions are coercive, oppressive, enslaving, imperialistic, dehumanising, subjugating, demonic and traumatic. In Salami-Agunloye's *The Queen Sisters*, Ubi observes that the oppression and dehumanisation of one is the same as that of many. Just like Sofola's Ogwoma, in *Wedlock of the Gods*, the feminist / womanist tendency is brought to an abrupt end whereby these female characters are unable to fulfil their struggles to freedom. Ogwoma dies and the struggle for self-assertiveness dies with her. Similarly, Ubi's banishment from the kingdom puts an end to female emancipation. While these two female characters have the capacities to change their immediate society, the struggles lead to their downfalls which take the readers back to culture. The two plays reveal that if socio-cultural values are not obeyed, the end is always disastrous.

At the expense of women's selfhood, they are to obey societal obligations that make them feel inferior to their male counterparts. However, through different writings, female creativities have helped to make women see their self-worth and the world in general sees the value of womanhood. While female creativity redresses the textual inferiority placed on women by making them the subjects rather than the objects, central eponymous character and to be the subject matter of discourse, unknowingly, some writers do not see it that way. They still view women from the 19th century perspectives whereby they are domesticated and husband lovers irrespective of the inhuman nature hurled on them.

Conclusion

Women writers are historians, recorders, teachers, projectors, preachers and interpreters of the same patriarchal societies that are often limiting their potentials. While these writers are not only seen as people who can change their situations within the public sphere, they are also self-examining the patriarchal societal values. However, some of the analysed Nigerian playwrights expose the male characters as selfish individuals who are rarely interested in the female's growth (educationally, physically, psychologically, economically and bodily), most of the female characters involved seem to be the harbinger of their own marginalisation.

Ironically, this is what is happening in Nigeria as women are agents perpetrating the removal of their own freedom. Nevertheless, women writers need to write more, showcase females' prowess and agility that they are ready to take up responsibilities in the public sphere. As such, women's lives should not be restricted to the domestic sphere which makes them voiceless, fragile, dependant, unassertive, redundant and useless. The negative images and status in their writings need to change as this will help send a message to the public that women are making their worth known instead of making their heroines die with their feminist / womanist struggles. Elevating the inner psyche and consciousness of female characters is very important as this will help in creating distinctively feminine nature and remove the inferiority complex of these characters.

REFERENCES

Achebe, C. (1989). *Arrow of God*. Lagos: Anchor Publishers.

Acholonu, C. (1994). *Motherism: The Afrocentric alternative to feminism*. Owerri: Afa Publications.

Afolabi, J. A. (2002). "Of womb-men, we-men, and woe-men: feminist aesthetics, theatre practice and democratic process in Nigeria", in Ahmed, Y. et al (eds.), *Theatre and democracy on Nigeria*. Ibadan: Kraft Books Limited, pp. 526-533.

Morgan, R. (1970). *Sisterhood is powerful: An anthology of writings from the women's liberation movement*. NYC 2970: Vintage Books

Nwapa, F. (2007). "Women and creative writing in Africa", in Olaniyan, T. & Quayson, A. (eds.), *African literature: An anthology of criticism and theory*. Oxford: Blackwell Publishing Ltd., pp. 526-533.

Obafemi, O. (1989). "Zulu Sofola's theatre: Nigerian female writers", in Otohumfor, H. & Nwodo, O. (eds.), *A critical perspective*. Lagos: Malthouse Press Ltd.

Okoh, J. (2003). *Cultural and women issues in Nigerian theatre and drama*. Owerri: Assumpta Press.

Okoh, J. (1997). *The Mannequins*. Owerri: Springfield Publishers.

Okoh, J. (2000). *Edewede*. Owerri: Totan Publishers.

Okoh, J. (2003). *Theatre and women's right in Nigeria*. Port Harcourt: Pearl Publishers.

Okoh, J. (2005). *Aisha*. Port Harcourt: Pearl Publishers.

Onwueme, T. (1992). *The reign of Wazobia and other plays*. Ibadan: Heinemann Educational Books.

Oyedepo, S. D. (2002). *The rebellion of the bumpy chested*. Ilorin: Delstar publishers.

Salami-Agunloye, I. I. (2011). *Challenging the master's craft: Women playwright in the theatre of men*. Boston: Evergreen Books.

Salami-Agunloye, I. I. (2002). *The Queen Sisters*. Jos: Saniez

Salami-Agunloye, I.I. (2003). *More than dancing*. Jos: Saniez

Showalter, E. (1986). *The new feminist criticism*. London: Virago Press Ltd.

Sofola, Z. (1972). *Wedlock of the gods*. Ibadan: Evan Books.

Sofola, Z. (1986). *The ivory tower*. Imprint: unpublished script.

Sofola, Z. (1974). *King Emene*. Ibadan: Heinemann Educational Books.

Sofola, Z. (1981). *Old wines are tasty*. Ibadan: Ibadan University press.

Solberg, R. (1981). *The women of Black Africa*. London: Routledge.

Stubbs, P. (1981). *Women and Fiction: Feminism and the Novel, 1880-1920*. London: Methuen and Co Ltd.

Utoh-Ezeajugh, T.C. (2011). "Out of the masks – A Play". *Matatu Journal of African Culture and Society: Spheres Public and Private-Western Genres in African Literature,* 39. Amsterdam & New York: Rodopi B.V. pp. 647-675

Walker, A. (1983). *In search of our mothers' gardens: Womanist prose*. Berkshire: Cox & Wyman Publishers.

NOTES ON CONTRIBUTORS

Rukayat ADEBIYI studied at the University of Ilorin, Kwara State, Nigeria where she obtained her BA and MA Degrees in Performing Arts. Her areas of interest in theatre scholarship are Theatre Business Management, Dramatic Theory and Criticism, and Playwriting.

Marian ADELOWO is a PhD student at the Department of the Performing Arts, University of Ilorin, Kwara State, Nigeria. Her area of interest is in Dramatic Theory and Criticism. She is also interested in interdisciplinary studies, which include gender studies, gay studies, and health humanities.

Oluwatomi ADEOTI teaches in the Department of English, Kwara State University, Malete, Nigeria. Her areas of research include Pragmatics, Cultural Studies, English Language Teaching (with focus on English as a Second Language), and Aviation English. She has published in both international and national books and journals.

Muftiat O. ADEYI is a dramatist and a playwright. Muftiat graduated from Kwara State University, Malete, Nigeria with BA in Performing Arts. She obtained her MA degree from the Department of the Performing Arts, University of Ilorin, Kwara, State, Nigeria.

Victoria A. ALABI is a Professor of English at the University of Ilorin, Nigeria. She is a member of the Nigerian Pragmatics Association.

Esther APATA is a lecturer at Kogi State University, Anyigba, Kogi State, Nigeria. She is completing her doctoral studies at the University of Ilorin, Nigeria on Dance Criticism and Performance Studies.

Adenike ARINOMO is a graduate of the Performing Arts Department, University of Ilorin, Ilorin, Nigeria. She taught Theatre Arts at the Federal College of Education (Special) Oyo. She is a literary analyst and specializes in Dramaturgy and Literary Criticism.

Bassey Nsa EKPE is a Lecturer with the Department of Performing Arts, Akwa Ibom State University, Nigeria. She is an alumnus of the University of Calabar where she obtained BA in Theatre Arts and MA in Media Studies. Bassey is a member of professional and learned societies. Her research interests are in Media Studies, Theatre / Cultural Studies, and Crossroads of Theatre and New Media.

Florence Adedoja ELEGBA is a Chief Lecturer of English Language, Communication in English, and Literature in English with the Department of Languages, School of General and Administrative Studies, The Federal Polytechnic, Idah, Kogi State, Nigeria. She is also a doctoral student with the Department of English, University of Ilorin, Ilorin. Her area of research interest is Dramatic Literature. She is the author of a novel titled *Beyond Disappointments*.

Oluwakemi M. EMMANUEL-OLOWONUBI lectures in the Department of English and Literary Studies, Federal University Lokoja, Kogi State, Nigeria. She is a critic and playwright. Her areas of research interest include Dramatic Criticism, and Gender and Cultural Studies. She is a member of the Society of Nigeria Theatre Artists (SONTA).

Lauretta IKE obtained her BA and MA in Performing Arts from University of Ilorin, Nigeria, with a thesis on 'Trauma Aesthetics and Emotional Recovery in Selected Nigerian Home Video Films'. Her research interests include Acting, Playwriting, Play

263

Directing, Dramatic Criticism and Film Studies. She has published scholarly articles in both local and international journals.

Oludolapo OJEDIRAN is a graduate of Performing Arts, University of Ilorin, Nigeria. She obtained her doctorate degree from Queen Margaret University, Edinburgh, United Kingdom where she specialized in Dramatic and Literary Criticism. Her interest is in Feminism / Womanism in Theatre, especially amongst African women. She currently lectures at The Performing Arts Department, University of Ilorin, Nigeria.

Hairat B. YUSUF is a versatile dancer who has taken part in different theatrical productions. She had her first and second degrees in Performing Arts at the University of Ilorin, Nigeria. She is currently a PhD student at Ahmadu Bello University, Zaria. Her research interests are Choreography and Dance Libretto writing. She lectures Dance and Choreography in the Department of Theatre and Performing Arts, Bayero University, Kano.

Index

266